Paths of the Western Sun
Volume II

View of Morro Rock from Black Hill

Mahmoud Shelton

The
Nine Sisters
of
California

Temple of Justice Books

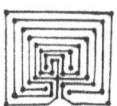

Copyright © 2023 D.M. Shelton

All rights reserved. This book or any portion thereof may not be reproduced or used in any manner whatsoever without the express written permission of the publisher.

templeofjustice@icloud.com

Printed in the United States of America

ISBN 978-0-9741468-7-4

Front cover: late Roman shield design of the *Mauri alites*
Back cover: panel from old Mission San Luis Obispo

"Don't become too proud of this technological terror you've spawned…The ability to destroy a city, a world, a whole system is still insignificant when set against the Force."

George Lucas
Star Wars: From the Adventures of Luke Skywalker, 1976

"Calafia Was Here"
Mural by Erin LeAnn Mitchell

CONTENTS

1	The Island of California	9
2	Mysteries of Nine	21
3	The Last Power	35
4	An Ancient Science	53
5	The Church with Two Naves	63
6	Devil Canyon	75
7	Custodians of Holy Lands	87
8	Occidentation	97

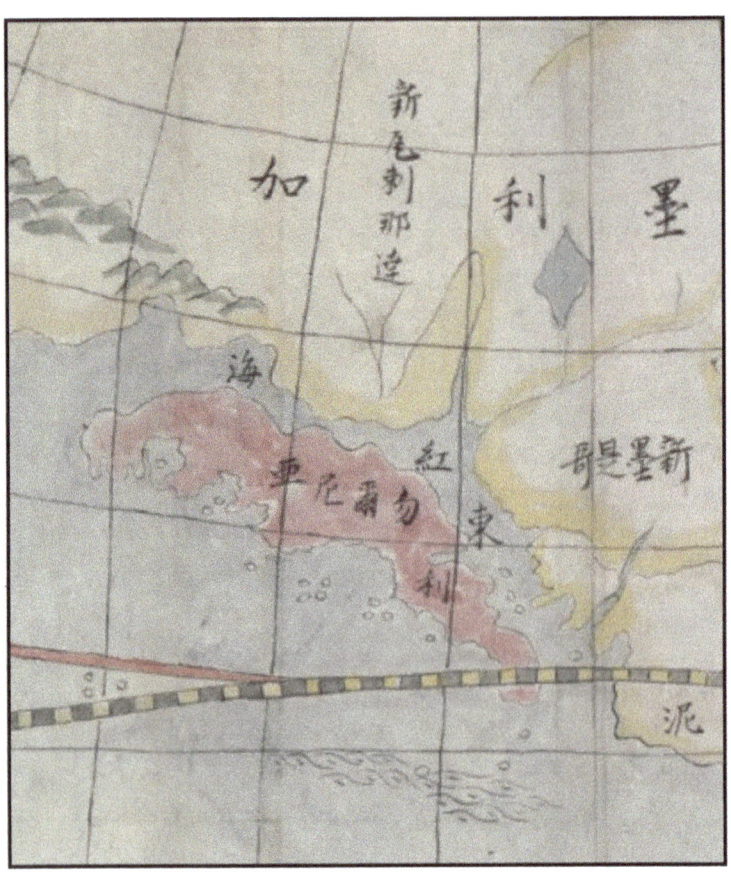

The Island of California
Map detail from 1865

1

The Island of California

Among the mysterious aspects of the modern state of California is its etymology. As I mentioned at the conclusion of my study *The Red and the White*,[1] the Spanish derived the name ultimately from the Arabic word *khilafah* for the supreme authority in Islam. The 16th century marked the fullest expansion of the Ottomans, who had inherited this authority or caliphate, and who were the greatest rivals of the Spanish empire in continental Europe. Surely not by accident, the name "California" emerges in the historical record in this same century, not long after the Spanish conquest of Mexico under Cortés. The etymology of this name, however, appears to have been only indirectly related to the authority held by the Ottomans, since it was lifted without alteration from a chivalric romance of the period. This is not surprising, since tales of chivalry remained popular, even more so for the Spanish conquistadors who dared venture beyond the Pillars of Hercules. Yet this particular romance, *Las Sergas de Esplandián* by Garci Rodríguez de Montalvo,[2] fell into obscurity following

---

[1] Temple of Justice Books, 2019.
[2] The origin of the name, albeit in a slightly different form, has been traced further still to *La Chanson de Roland* of the 11th century.

its appearance in 1510, being a lesser-known continuation or "fifth book" of the popular adventures of Esplandián's father, Amadís of Gaul. What is more, the Medieval ideal of chivalry was beginning to fade, and by the 17th century its loss would be acknowledged by Cervantes above all, who even disparages Esplandián specifically.[3] The etymology of California was therefore long overlooked, until Edward E. Hale discovered its proper origin in 1862.

In chapter 157 of *Las Sergas de Esplandián*, the reader is offered a description of the land called California:

> Know, then, that, on the right hand of the Indies, there is an island called California, very close to the site of the Terrestrial Paradise, and it was peopled by black women, without any man among them, for they lived in the fashion of Amazons…Their island was the strongest in all the world, with its steep cliffs and rocky shores. Their arms were all of gold, and so was the harness of the wild beasts they rode. For, in the whole island, there was no metal but gold…They had many ships with which they sailed out to other countries to obtain booty.
>
> In this island, called California, there were many griffins, on account of the great ruggedness of the country…Every man who landed on the island was immediately devoured by these griffins…[4]

It is not known whether Cortés was familiar with *Las Sergas de Esplandián* in particular, but he does express in his letters a belief

---

[3] See chapter 6 of *Don Quixote*.
[4] Translation by Hale in "The Queen of California," *His Level Best and Other Stories*, Boston: Roberts Brothers, 1885, pages 245-6.

in the land of Amazons.⁵ In a similar manner, an awareness of the Terrestrial Paradise haunted the voyages of the European explorers, including those of Columbus, and Hale addresses this theme following his study on the source for the name California. He points out that the belief in the antipodal location of the Terrestrial Paradise was a legacy of the cosmology of Dante's *Divine Comedy*. What Hale is unable to appreciate is how the association between the Terrestrial Paradise and the etymology of California accords with Islamic doctrine. Very specifically, the establishment of the first human presence on Earth is expressed in the Holy Qur'an in terms of a "caliphate."⁶

More generally, the mythological elements in the above passage belong to a Medieval language of romance comprehensible to all the Abrahamic traditions. For example, there are elements here shared with what is surely the greatest of these romances in East and West, that of Alexander the Great. Not surprisingly, given the ancient subject matter of the Alexander Romance, these elements may be traced back well before the Middle Ages. Concerning the griffins that play such a key role in Montalvo's account, Pliny the Elder had in Classical antiquity noted an important indication of their symbolism when he described that their nests contained gold nuggets. Among metals, gold corresponds to the Sun, and a griffin was formulated as a hybrid of lion and eagle which are both symbolically solar. Griffins are therefore in perfect keeping with the symbolism of a land with "no metal but gold." Even before Pliny the Elder, the Greek authority Herodotus places griffins in a significant geographical context, since he specifies that the

---

⁵ This belief may not have been entirely misplaced, since in 1605, the first myth recorded from Native California described a settlement exclusively of women upon the island of Santa Catalina (Harrington, "Indian Words in Southwest Spanish, Exclusive of Proper Nouns," *Plateau*, volume 17 number 2, October 1944, page 35).
⁶ II, 30.

land of the griffins borders the land of the Hyperboreans. For the ancient Greeks, the Hyperboreans were the people of the earliest age of the world, and this age was termed golden. Here again, we discover an association with gold; and while the Classical Golden Age is surely synonymous with the Terrestrial Paradise, it should not be forgotten that Montalvo's California is only "close" to the paradisal land and not to be identified with that land itself. As for the devouring griffins, they are obviously a formulation of the "Guardians of the Sundoor" who bar the entrance to Paradise.[7]

Episode from the Medieval Romance of Alexander the Great

---

[7] Cf. *Guardians of the Sundoor: Late Iconographic Essays and Drawings of Ananda K. Coomaraswamy*, edited by Robert A. Strom, Louisville: Fons Vitae, 2004.

The Island of California

To understand the indications in Montalvo's account, we are provided incomparable help by the writings of René Guénon on the symbolism of temporal cycles. Guénon preferred the use of the term "Hyperborean" for the primordial tradition of the Golden Age, at least in part because it emphasizes the northern orientation of that tradition. This "polar" emphasis he considers to have precedence over the solar orientation that came to succeed it.[8] Consistent with his use of the Classical term for the Primordial Tradition, and following Plato, Guénon used the word "Atlantean" to describe the secondary development that was focused upon the West rather than the North, and that emphasized royal virtues over those of the sacerdotal caste.[9] We in fact find this last indication well represented in *Las Sergas de Esplandián*, of course, and the description of the "many ships with which they sailed out to other countries to obtain booty" recalls Plato's description of Atlantis. Now, the supreme land in the North was sometimes described as an island, such as the island of Thule, but it is above all Atlantis that provides the model of an island "strongest in all the world." Any secondary traditional center may be said to occupy a position "close" to the Terrestrial Paradise, since it serves as a visible approximation of a reality that has become unseen; but here we may recognize in Montalvo's description of California the memory of the island of Atlantis. That the Spanish should name a land far across the Atlantic based on that memory is somehow in agreement with Dr. John Dee's observation made on behalf of Spain's rival in the New World: "the ancient Atlantis, no longer – nowe named America."[10] Without disputing what Dr. Dee really meant by

---

[8] Cf. volume I of *Paths of the Western Sun* (*Ancient Secrets of the Rogue Valley*, Temple of Justice Books, 2022), page 73.

[9] Guénon regards the warrior caste as "feminine" in relation to the sacerdotal.

[10] Cf. *The Red and the White: Perspectives on America and the Primordial Tradition*, op. cit., page 7.

this, the end of the Atlantean era came long before the Age of Discovery, and it is significant that besides its mythological associations with vanished sacred centers, California should be named after the highest living authority at the time of its discovery.[11]

In accordance with its mythological inspirations, California was long believed to be in fact an island, at least according to the cartographic evidence from all parts of the world (see the Oriental example on page 8). Modern opinion prefers to regard this persistent depiction as an error deriving from extrapolating the shape of the Baja Peninsula that first bore the name "California." Only rarely is Montalvo's idea considered in this context. Of course, as an idea, it might be offered that California is even today recognized as a "land apart," at least politically, and so it is worth defining the extent of the "island" of California, at least conceptually. To begin with, California is more than the modern state in America, for that state succeeds only the Spanish designation of Alta or Upper California in relation to Baja or Lower California. Uniting these two Californias was the mission system of the Spanish Empire. The establishment of the missions in Baja California commenced in 1683 under the direction of the Jesuits, but their expulsion in 1768 demonstrated the Spanish tendency to disregard the proper relationship of royal power to sacerdotal authority. As a consequence, however, the missions of Alta California arose under the direction of the Franciscan Order beginning in 1769. The establishing of the missions in two phases may therefore be understood to prefigure the eventual separation of the two Californias.[12]

---

[11] Even in the Age of Chivalry, the Caliphate was recognized as the "supreme power on Earth," at least according to Wolfram von Eschenbach's *Parzival*.

[12] With the Franciscans focused in Alta California, the Dominican Order was chosen to oversee the missions of Baja California.

Better than any other political development, the missions may be considered to have defined California, at least for the people who named it; but if the missions were naturally limited in their southern extent by the geography of the Baja Peninsula, how far north did they reach? Officially the northernmost mission is in Sonoma, but it was built after the Mexican War of Independence and so never belonged to the Spanish Empire; moreover, the mission only functioned for 11 years. The next official mission to the south was in San Rafael, but it was built as a sanitarium and only secondarily became a mission. It lasted longer than the Sonoma mission, but more than any other it was destroyed by history, although a replica of the mission chapel was built in 1949 and remains on the original site.[13] It could easily be maintained, then, that the Imperial mission system extended to the San Francisco Bay and no further, which is very conveniently in perfect harmony with a historic British claim. The name of Drake's Bay just north of San Francisco commemorates Sir Francis Drake's supposed landing in 1579, when he claimed New Albion for the British Empire.[14] Of course, by the time of the missions, it was rather the Russian Empire that presented an obstacle against Spain's expansion further north. Regardless, the Adams-Onís treaty of 1819 limited Spanish interests at the 42nd parallel, and this limit was preserved as the northern border of the state of California; but to conceptualize the "island of California," it seems more important to consider the de facto extent of Spanish influence.

---

[13] For the map on page 16, Sonoma and San Rafael are represented by open circles.

[14] Drake's Bay remains the most likely candidate for the place of his landing, even without the false "Drake's Plate" fabricated by members of the fraternal parody called "E Clampus Vitus." Confirmation would seem to have been found in the form of an Elizabethan silver coin minted in 1567 that was unearthed at the nearby Native site known as Olompali.

The Nine Sisters of California

Spanish mission locations
upon the ancient "island" of California

The Island of California

    This concept is rather neatly supported by evidence of the region's prehistoric geography. California's interior to the east of the northernmost missions is now part of the Central Valley, but geologists refer to its ancient identity as Lake Corcoran, a massive body of water that would have rivalled the modern Great Lakes. In the south of California near the border with Mexico, another large and ancient lake, now referred to as Lake Cahuilla, would have further isolated western California from the rest of the continent. Scientists insist that these waters had dramatically diminished long before historic times, but even after the Spanish period, a map of California from 1830 included a body of water labelled "Cienegas de Tulares"[15] that very closely approximated the dimensions of the ancient Lake Corcoran. Be that as it may, these ancient wetlands would very swiftly be unmade in the modern era; but before the transformation of California's interior through water reclamation projects and years of extreme water consumption and drought, it would not have been inconceivable to experience the chain of missions through Baja and Alta California as occupying a land more or less surrounded by water, especially in years of more pronounced seasonal flooding. Despite the burdens of modern agriculture, seasonal flooding in 2023 witnessed the return of Lake Tulare, part of the Cienegas de Tulares, which brought tremendous losses to the agricultural industry. The return of Lake Tulare is simply a reassertion of the natural balance of things.[16]

---

[15] It is worth noting the use here of the word "Tule," that I have elsewhere associated with the naming of sacred centers (see *The Red and the White*, op. cit., page 18).

[16] Even so, scientific opinion was quick to insist that such flooding is insufficient to reverse chronic drought; but with statements comparable to those addressing the Klamath water crisis (see "The Klamath Balance" in *Guardians of the Heart: Essays in Sacred Geography*, Temple of Justice Books, 2022), scientists admit that seasonal flooding would be more beneficial without the levee systems that have drained the

Aside from these considerations, the California Gold Rush seems to offer the clearest historical confirmation of the relevance of Montalvo's original mythology. By 1849, however, the two Californias had been sundered; and if Montalvo insists on the incomparability of his island stronghold, the Gold Rush proved that California's integrity was all too vulnerable to invasion, ecological destruction, and genocide. Besides, it is curious that the historical gold fields lie outside our conceptualization of the island of California. Nevertheless, the designation "Golden State" no doubt echoes Montalvo's description, even if California became part of the United States in 1850 rather than exist apart.

○

The cataclysm suffered by the Native populations of California necessarily involved their sacred landscapes. From its beginnings with the Spanish, it would only make sense for the invaders to occupy the places where Native culture was already focused. As part of the legacy of Cortés, the church constructed atop the pyramid at Cholula in Mexico is an obvious example, and the ancient importance of the site may be surmised by the artificial hill's incomparable immensity. John Michell cites the responsibility of conquerors to preserve from the conquered "the seasons proper for invoking the fertilizing influences and of the sacred spots appropriate for that purpose,"[17] but the evidence for this in the Spanish conquest is far from

---

wetlands. In other words, only now are conditions becoming dire enough for scientists to admit the culpability of their engineering predecessors.

[17] *The New View Over Atlantis*, San Francisco: Harper & Row, 1983, page 199.

overwhelming. The Day of the Dead celebrations in Mexico are often cited as an example of pre-Columbian culture that survived the conquest; however, the timing of these celebrations is out of keeping with Native tradition, since it is presumed that the Aztecs chose the summer for their analogous commemorations.[18] That some sort of continuity with ancient tradition was preserved under the Spanish should not simply be assumed.

The mission of San Luis Obispo in Alta California[19] was built along a chain of volcanic plugs or lava necks that are now known as the Nine Sisters, or the Morros. The last of these peaks that rises from the sea at Morro Bay, El Morro or Morro Rock, is the source of this designation, with the word "morro" here signifying a rounded headland.[20] Before a modern causeway was constructed through the quarrying of the rock itself, Morro Rock would have been separated from the shore with the tides. Not surprisingly, given the greatness of the isolated rocky dome, Morro Rock figures as a sacred location in Native lore. The Spanish supposedly called this sacred peak a "moro" originally, in reference to the tall helmets of the Moors or Spanish Muslims. The etymologies of "morro" and "moro" are really indistinguishable. The Iberian word "morro" seems to be applied to a headland precisely because of its fortified character, and there remain to this day Moorish castles throughout Spain and Portugal. We should recognize that this name comes from the same chivalric context from which the name "California" was taken. Now, the word "Moor" may be traced further to

---

[18] Somewhat ironically, the Catholic choice of a cross-quarter day of autumn for its observances is presumably a legacy of pre-Christian European tradition.

[19] For the map on page 16, Mission San Luis Obisbo de Tolosa is represented by the red circle.

[20] "Morro" in Spanish may also mean "nose," based on a different etymology.

Roman use and relates to the Greek word *mauros* for "black." Here, then, we are even closer to Montalvo's vision, since his Californians were specifically black. Despite the ultimate Islamic source of the word "California," however, this is not to suggest that these warriors were Moors in the religious sense. In *Las Sergas de Esplandián*, the Queen of California, named Calafia, is independent from the communities of Muslims and Christians in the story and chooses to side with one before the other. For Montalvo, blackness reinforces the exotic and powerful identity of the queen and her warriors.

Situated alongside the mission, the San Luis Obispo Museum of Art in 2022 unveiled its second annual mural project, entitled "Calafia Was Here." This contemporary revival of her memory is by no means an isolated example. In 2021, to mention but another very recent example, a live performance of her return to California soil was staged in Sausalito on San Francisco Bay, and this performance suggested an act of sympathetic magic. What is consistent in all such depictions is an insistence on connecting the name of the state with the queen alone, rather than recognize that her name is presumably a title – like caliph - deriving imaginatively from the name of her island. There is, in fact, a reason for this insistence, for the mythic image of a queen and her female companions living magically apart may be traced far beyond Montalvo, and even beyond the Classical legend of Amazons. The relevance of Queen Calafia in San Francisco is clear enough, since it recalls the limit of Spanish California as we have seen, but the presence of Calafia is especially meaningful in a landscape dominated by Nine Sisters.

2

Mysteries of Nine

According to Montalvo, Queen Calafia and her companions "lived in the fashion of Amazons," but he does not insist that they were Amazons in actuality. Indeed, the Classical legend that was passed down to the Age of Chivalry never situated their home upon an island. We should therefore ignore the specific associations of the word "Amazon" that do not apply here, and consider other legendary precursors to a community composed solely of females. From Ancient China comes the account of the Buddhist traveler Hui Shen, who included a description of a "Land of Women" located just beyond the land of Fusang. As I have addressed elsewhere, there is a preponderance of evidence indicating that Fusang must be identified with the West Coast of North America.[21] Western studies on the subject of Fusang have presumed that the voyage of Hui Shen involved a passage down the Pacific coast, and have generally sought to associate Fusang with Mexico. However, European maps of the 18th century position Fusang further north in lands never claimed by Spain, and if this earlier interpretation

---

[21] See chapter 7 of *The Red and the White*.

is correct, California would correspond to the Land of Women.[22] The legends of Spain and of China are in strange agreement, then, concerning the mythic identity of California.[23]

Another meaningful analogue to Montalvo's imagery may be found closer to the legendry of Medieval Spain. In his *History of the Kings of Britain* and the later *Life of Merlin*, Geoffrey of Monmouth describes Nine Sisters of Avalon who, like Montalvo's Californians, live upon an island and whose female company is ruled by a queen. This queen is known from the wider Arthurian cycle as Morgan le Fay, and she appears first in the writings of Geoffrey. Curiously, despite her depiction as an evil sorceress throughout Arthurian legend, she first plays a perfectly benevolent role as caretaker to the wounded King Arthur.[24] This ambivalence is, however, akin to that of Queen Calafia, who, as mentioned above, turned from opposing to supporting Christian chivalry.

While it will be admitted that these sisters of Avalon are not warriors, we do however find this attribute in another formulation of Nine Sisters within the same cycle of tales. In the Welsh legend of Peredur that is part of the *Mabinogion*, the hero must face the Nine Witches of Caer Lloyw. Even though Arthur and his knights ultimately destroy these terrible opponents, there is an ambivalence even here, for Peredur was in fact

---

[22] In *The Red and the White*, I compared the Redwood tree of California with the solar tree of Fusang (page 74); but if the geography of our island of California is equated with the Land of Women south of Fusang, it is worth observing that the vast majority of Redwood trees would in fact belong to the land north of this Land of Women.

[23] "California girls" remains an idea in the popular consciousness focused on Southern California, and so on the middle of the legendary island.

[24] This benevolent role of the Queen of Avalon is somewhat surprisingly preserved in the late compilation of Sir Thomas Malory. Compare also her mysterious participation in *Sir Gawain and the Green Knight*.

tutored by the witches in the more arcane arts of war. This valuable knowledge is therefore passed on to Peredur. What is more, the name of their stronghold Caer Lloyw means the "Glowing Castle," and so a luminous aspect is present. Now, the idea of a military stronghold or castle for a group of nine sisters or maidens is an insistent one, as we find "Castles of Maidens" in folklore both within and outside of Europe. As a recurring motif of Arthurian romance, a Castle of Maidens usually appears in the context of the adventures of the hero Gawain specifically. Sometimes this folklore becomes attached to specific geographical sites, such as Edinburgh Castle in Scotland. Perched upon the lava neck of Castle Hill, this fortress was once known as the Castle of the Maidens, and these maidens were presumably but another formulation of the Nine Sisters.

When considering the Celtic milieu, it is important to recall the words of René Guénon concerning the meaning of the name "Avalon:" "it is clearly identical to *Ablun* or *Belen*, that is, of the Celtic and Hyperborean Apollo, so that the Isle of Avalon is yet another name for the 'solar land;' which at a certain time moreover was transported symbolically from the north to the west, in correspondence with one of the principal changes that occurred in the different traditional forms in the course of our Manvantara."[25] Guénon is referring at the end of the quote primarily to the Atlantean tradition, and we have already had reason to consider the participation of California in its symbolism, only now it is possible to identify California as another "solar land," or rather another land modelled upon the true "solar land" that is ordinarily inaccessible. As far as Apollo is concerned, it is remarkable indeed that nine sisters are

---

[25] "The Land of the Sun," *Symbols of Sacred Science*, Hillsdale: Sophia Perennis, 2004, pages 92-3. With the term "Manvantara," Guénon is referring to the Hindu doctrine of temporal cycles that he preferred for its precision.

specifically attached to his function in the form of the Nine Muses. Geoffrey of Monmouth actually provides names for his sisters of Avalon, and it is surely not by accident that some of these names suggest a Greek origin. Another detail that Geoffrey provides likewise recalls the Muses, since he mentions a sister named Thitis who was distinguished by her skill with the "cither," that is, a musical instrument. Of course, the word music itself derives from the Muses,[26] though each of the sisters was the patron of a specific art, of which music was but one. Epic poetry, history, comedy, tragedy, dance, lyric poetry, sacred poetry, and astronomy were all under the authority of the Muses. Taken together, it was their function in society to oversee the inspiration of the soul through these arts, and an emphasis on the oral transmission of knowledge betrays their ancient character.[27]

The peaks in and around San Luis Obispo presently called the Nine Sisters were not always known as such. It is unclear whether Native tradition or the Spanish identified their number. In terms of geology, there are many more than nine landforms that could be counted; but just as cities are claimed to have seven hills in order to partake in the archetype of Rome, there is an archetype of nine sisters to which these hills conform. Neither is it clear where the inspiration to call them "sisters" came from, unless we recall that A.B. Cook more than a century ago derived the name "Muse" from "mountain:" "This derivation (which occurred independently to Dr. Giles, to myself, and doubtless to others also) is suggested by the fact that

---

[26] The word "museum" also derives from the Muses.
[27] The Parisian Lodge of the Nine Sisters to which Benjamin Franklin belonged was named for the Muses, and the unorthodox character of Franklin's Masonry provides another example of the ambivalence attached to our subject.

Landscape with Apollo and the Muses
Claude Lorrain, 1652

all the most important cult-centres of the Muses were on mountains or hills."[28]

☉

A circle with a point at its center is the symbol traditionally shared by gold and the Sun, and René Guénon has included it among the symbols of the "Heart of the

---

[28] *Zeus: Study in Ancient Religion*, volume I, Cambridge: Cambridge University Press, 1914, page 104.

World." His analysis of its numerical significance is especially pertinent here:

> In the science of numbers, it is the symbol of the denary insofar as this constitutes a complete numerical cycle; from this point of view, the center is 1 and the circumference 9, totaling together 10, for unity, being the very principle of numbers, must be placed at the center and not on the circumference, whose natural measure, moreover, is not accomplished by decimal division...but by division by the multiples of 3, 9, and 12.[29]

Guénon's contemporary continuator, Charles-André Gilis, has explained further that this geometry demonstrates the feminine aspect of the number 9.[30] The mythology of the Nine Sisters does include circularity, as may be seen in the stone circles and hill forts of ancient Europe. In Cornwall, for example, there are stone circles called the Merry Maidens and Nine Maidens, and the latter is so named despite being comprised of more stones than nine. Of course, neither are such monuments necessarily exact circles. The rounded hill forts of England are also repeatedly named Maiden Castle, and this may very well be connected to the Irish belief that the ancient ringforts belong to the fairies. After all, the Queen of the Nine Sisters is better known as

---

[29] *The Great Triad*, Hillsdale: Sophia Perennis, 2001, pages 140-1. In the example of the Muses, it is clear that Apollo may be identified as their spiritual "principle." It should not be overlooked that the Pythagoreans, who believed that their founder had a direct relationship with Apollo, placed great importance on the denary, although it was arranged instead in the triangular form of the Tetraktys (see page 98).

[30] *La Petite fille de neuf ans*, Paris: Le Turban Noir, 2006, page 16. The warrior aspect of the Nine Sisters is not unrelated to the feminine character of knightly power in relation to spiritual authority.

Whereas most megalithic monuments known as Nine Sisters are circular, this example from Cornwall is a linear stone row.

Morgan *le Fay*, that is, the Fairy. In an early version of the Grail quest, King Arthur launches a raid into the Underworld to obtain the cauldron of Annwn, a sort of circular talisman, and the Welsh account relates a mysterious detail: "By the breath of nine maidens was it kindled." [31]

Elsewhere I have addressed the ontological relationship between the Underworld and the fairies, a subject clarified only by recourse to the Islamic conception of the jinn.[32] The root of the Arabic word *j-n-n* relates to "hiddenness," a characteristic shared both by the Underworld and the fairies, but it is specifically owing to their intermediate cosmic rank that this relationship belongs. According to Islamic cosmology, the jinn occupy a position between the luminous angels and material humanity, though like human beings the jinn have the freedom to choose their allegiances. Similarly, the Underworld is in some

---

[31] John and Caitlin Matthews, *King Arthur's Raid on the Underworld: The Oldest Grail Quest*, Glastonbury: Gothic Image Publications, 2008, pages 58-9. Recalling the Amazons especially, the authors in their commentary include a reference to a Celtic sisterhood "who live fiercely apart from men, although they visit men in order to engender children."

[32] See *The Red and the White*, page 41.

sense intermediate between the spiritual and terrestrial realms. For the human microcosm, the analogous position belongs to the soul (*nafs*) between the spirit (*rūh*) and body (*jism*). Now, it is worth considering that the word here for soul, *nafs*, is essentially the same as the word for breath (*nafas*), indicating a concept found worldwide, such as with the Chinese concept of *chi*. For this reason, the "breath of the nine maidens" may be recognized as an indication of their cosmic rank. It is also worth comparing in this context the Queen of Avalon with the most renowned and honored queen in Islam. The story of the Queen of Sheba is told in the Holy Qur'an,[33] and includes the inadvertent display of her feet that commentators describe as having a strange appearance; "later Moslem writers interpreted this physical peculiarity as showing that she was of jinn descent."[34]

    Having established that the circularity of the Nine Sisters' stronghold is in keeping with the science of numbers, it is worth acknowledging a famous example of the soul imagined as a circular castle,[35] especially since this example is linked to the milieu of Spanish chivalry. Among the treasures of Spanish Catholicism is the *Interior Castle* of Santa Teresa that describes the soul as a castle of seven concentric rings. Teresa was born in 1515 in the walled city known as "Ávila of the Knights," "Ávila of the Loyal Ones," the "Town of Stone and Saints." Not too surprisingly, before joining the Carmelite Order, she was inspired by the tales of chivalry of her time, including Garci Rodríguez de Montalvo's tales of Amadís and Espandián;[36] and

---

[33] XXVII, 22-44.

[34] C.H. Toy, "The Queen of Sheba," *The Journal of American Folklore*, volume 20, number 78, American Folklore Society, July-September 1907, page 211.

[35] Recall also the circularity of the city of Atlantis.

[36] Cf. Paul Morris, "Lonesome Knights of a Spanish Nun: Teresa of Ávila and Chivalresque Literature in Sixteenth-Century Spain," *Anistoriton Journal*, volume 9, December 2005.

just as the name "California" betrays the influence of Islam, the circular castle of Santa Teresa is clearly anticipated by the schema of Islamic esoterism. Miguel Asín Palacios, the Catholic scholar who revealed that Dante's *Divine Comedy* owed a profound debt to Islam, proposed that a similar case should be made for the *Interior Castle*; yet it is thanks to the more recent work of Luce López Baralt that the depth of Santa Teresa's antecedents may be appreciated.[37] Baralt refers to the *Haft Paykar* of Nizami as prefiguring the structure of Santa Teresa's castle,[38] and this comparison is important for a number of reasons that concern us here. To begin with, since Nizami's seven domes relate at once to the microcosm of the soul and the planetary spheres of the macrocosm, the sphericity or circularity of the soul's castle is perfectly comprehensible. What is more, Nizami arranges a group of "seven princesses," one for each dome, to serve as living embodiments of the seven spheres.

Of course, given the ubiquitous importance of the septenary,[39] it would seem that this last observation is irrelevant to a grouping of nine. However, there is a traditional understanding of the cosmos that posits exactly nine planets, an understanding that is at least mimicked by the modern materialistic tally. In Hinduism specifically, besides the seven planets of the Ptolemaic system, there are two planets that are not distant as in modern cosmology, but rather relate to the very

---

[37] "Santa Teresa and Islamic Mysticism: The Symbol of the Seven Castles of the Soul," *Islam in Spanish Literature: From the Middle Ages to the Present*, translated by Andrew Hurley, Leiden: Brill, 1992, page 119. A noteworthy subsequent example may be found in the visionary lotus castle of Rōshi Jiyu Kennett that significantly has nine towers (*How to Grow a Lotus Blossom or How a Zen Buddhist Prepares for Death*, Mt. Shasta: Shasta Abbey, 1977).

[38] Ibid., pages 116-9.

[39] Cf. *Sacred Geography and the Paths of the Sun* (Temple of Justice Books, 2021) pages 9-11, especially concerning the categorization of the planets as an intermediary domain.

immediate concern of the eclipses; and unlike the planetary luminaries, these two are not luminous but dark. Together the nine planets are the Navagraha, and are classically depicted as nine figures. In the example above the two at the far right display the demonic head and ophidian body that identify them as Rahu and Ketu. Their mythological origin is traced to the creation of *amrita*, or "Water of Life," during the "Churning of the Sea of Milk," when a demonic *asura* stole a taste of the *amrita* and so attained immortality, yet was sundered in two for his crime. Thereafter, the head Rahu and body Ketu have always sought vengeance by eclipsing the lights of the Sun and Moon.

In a remarkable article published in 1938 and dedicated to Ananda Coomaraswamy, Willy Hartner reviewed the astronomical interpretation of Rahu and Ketu as the pseudoplanetary nodes of the Moon's orbit.[40] More importantly, Hartner demonstrated the presence of these "pseudoplanets" in Hindu and Islamic iconographies. The perpetuation of these two demonic figures within Islam is all the more intriguing since, as

---

[40] Willy Hartner, "The Pseudoplanetary Nodes of the Moon's Orbit in Hindu and Islamic Iconographies," *Ars Islamica*, volume 5 number 2, Washington: Freer Gallery et al., 1938.

the author reminds us, Muslim authorities were well aware that "they are no real planets."[41] Rahu and Ketu are known in Islam as the head and tail of the dragon, although the lunar nodes could alternatively be depicted as a two-headed dragon or snake.[42] The presence of dragon symbolism here only confirms the ambivalent character of our subject. Hartner dares go further in his study and provides an "excursus" on the incorporation of traditional motifs identifying the pseudoplanets in the Gundestrup Cauldron of the Celtic tradition. With this evidence, it seems that the formulation of nine planets is not irrelevant to the milieu to which the Nine Maidens and the Queen of Avalon belong; and we have already noted the relevance of astronomy to the Nine Muses.

The example of the pseudoplanetary nodes provides proof of the respect Islam historically accorded the arcane lore of India. Another example is to be found in the various versions

The Ottoman *Matali` us-sa`dah* embellishes the ancient symbol 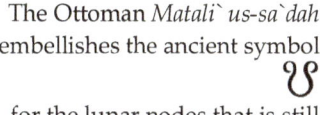 for the lunar nodes that is still in use in modern astronomy.

---

[41] Biruni (ibid., page 133).

[42] Concerning the ophidian form, it is worth noting that the jinn are thought to take corporeal form most commonly as serpents (cf. Charles-André Gilis, *Aperçus sur la Doctrine Akbarienne des Jinns*, Beirut: Albouraq, 2005, page 90).

of the Tantric *Pool of Amrita* text that have appeared throughout the lands of Islam, even within Sufi Orders of the Ottoman Empire.[43] Among the subjects of this text are the female spirits known as yoginis, who are believed to inhabit specific places on the Indian landscape. While the number of them varies, it is significant that they are sometimes counted as nine. What is more, as a group of seven they are placed in correspondence with the planets, and in microcosmic terms, the subtle centers called chakras;[44] yet in at least one version of the text, there are actually nine chakras.[45] This calculation only confirms the significance of nine in the science of numbers, since the literal meaning of chakra is "circle." As a group, however, the chakras are arranged along the sagittal axis of the human body, and we will return to a macrocosmic example of a nine-fold alignment. For now, it is enough to observe that the nine chakras and planets naturally correspond to the group of nine yoginis.

Before proceeding, it is worth mentioning another example of the close relationship between formulations of seven and nine. Worldwide, the asterism of the Great Bear or Dipper is quite naturally envisioned as a group of seven stars, yet this is not the case in the Chinese tradition: "The Nine Stars are the stars in the Constellation of the Dipper plus two neighboring stars. In Taoism the Nine Stars are the home of deities that

---

[43] The Greatest Master of Islamic esoterism Ibn ʿArabi from Spain has even been claimed as the author of the text, for reasons I have addressed elsewhere (see the chapter "Buddislam?" in *Mysteries of Dune: Sufism, Psychedelics, and the Prediction of Frank Herbert*, Temple of Justice Books, 2020).

[44] For a chart of correspondences, see Carl W. Ernst, "The Islamization of Yoga in the Amrtakunda Translations," *Journal of the Royal Asiatic Society*, Cambridge University Press, July 2003.

[45] Because the number 360 is but a multiple of 9, with the factor 40 representing completion, this doctrine of nine centers might reasonably be compared to the teaching found in the Traditions of the Prophet of Islam that the human physiognomy includes a total of 360 "joints."

control the destiny of humanity." This last significance corresponds to the most ancient Hindu understanding, according to which this asterism was the home of the Rishis before their shift to the Pleiades; and Islamic esoterism offers a more or less equivalent teaching.[46] What is even more remarkable about the Chinese insistence on nine stars is that in feng-shui, popularly called Chinese geomancy, "the Nine Stars are used to describe the shape of mountains."[47]

These arcane matters are well beyond the concerns of modern people who might refer to a chain of peaks as the Nine Sisters. So also for modern followers of Islam, it is beyond comprehension that "access to the female spirits called *joginis* (yoginis) was considered useful by Muslim rulers on military expeditions in Gujerat in the late sixteenth century."[48] Usefulness in war clearly recalls the martial prowess of the Nine Witches of Welsh legend, yet such analogies between the yoginis of traditional India and the Nine Sisters of ancient Europe have gone unrecognized. It should not be assumed, however, that these analogies are attributable to a diffusion of Indian doctrine. It is far more likely that we are dealing here with a very ancient theme indeed, shared by myriad traditional forms that all emerged in the postdiluvian world.[49] Because of

---

[46] On the shifting of the Rishis, see René Guénon, *The King of the World*, Hillsdale: Sophia Perennis, 2001, chapter 10; on the Great Bear in Islamic esoterism, see Henry Corbin, *The Man of Light in Iranian Sufism*, Boulder: Shambhala, 1978, pages 52-5.

[47] Quotations are from Eva Wong, *Feng-shui: The Ancient Wisdom of Harmonious Living for Modern Times*, Boston: Shambhala, 1996, page 76.

[48] Carl W. Ernst, "Being Careful with the Goddess: Yoginis in Persian and Arabic Texts" in *Performing Ecstasy: The Poetics and Politics of Religion in India*, Manohar Publishers, 2009.

[49] On the Atlantean tradition and postdiluvian traditional forms, see *The Red and the White*, especially chapter 2. It should also be noted that the inspired fantasy of Professor Tolkien concerns the establishing of such a postdiluvian tradition, and that nine were the number of sailing ships

the antiquity of this mythic power and its associations with the intermediary world of the soul, its ambiguity is among its defining characteristics, and for "one to whom this door is opened," according to a version of the *Pool of Amrita*, "if he is good, he will be a saint, and if he is evil, he will be a sorcerer."[50]

---

that carried the Faithful from Tolkien's Atlantis or "Atalantë," to the west of which was his Avalon or "Avallónë;" and nine were the "Witch-king" and his fellows who opposed that tradition (on these examples and the symbolism of 9, see *Alchemy in Middle-earth: The Significance of J.R.R. Tolkien's The Lord of the Rings*, Temple of Justice Books, 2003).

[50] Ernst 2003. I prefer the word "sorcerer" here to Ernst's "magician," since the latter's root meaning includes wisdom and so is ill-suited to contrast completely with "saint." These two contrasting possibilities likewise pertain to the "Science of Letters" of Islamic esoterism according to Muhyiddin Ibn `Arabi, and it is worth repeating here that Shaykh Muhyiddin has even been claimed as the author of the *Pool of Amrita* (see *Mysteries of Dune,* op. cit.; on the Science of Letters, see below).

3

The Last Power

From the ethnographic evidence, the Morros or Nine Sisters between San Luis Obispo and Morro Bay represent a border between two distinct Native peoples, the Chumash to the south and Salinan[51] to the north. For the former, Morro Rock was called Lisamu', while for the Salinan, the sacred dome was Lesámù, and so both peoples knew the peak by the same name; indeed, Edward Sapir classified the languages of these peoples as both belonging to the Hokan language family. Academics since Alfred Kroeber consider the Northern Chumash to be the traditional inhabitants of Morro Bay, and while Salinan peoples are associated with Mission San Miguel and Mission San Antonio to the north of San Luis Obispo, the latter mission presumably ministered especially to the Chumash. Archaeologists accordingly presume that the Native sites between San Luis Obispo and Morro Rock are to be attributed to that group. However, the Native lore about the Nine Sisters that has been recorded has come overwhelmingly from Salinan

---

[51] As with so many tribal designations, the name "Salinan" has no traditional relevance, deriving simply from the non-Native name for the Salinas River.

sources. Making assumptions concerning the prehistory of the landscape is by no means straightforward.[52]

For example, Salinan sources speak of a sea turtle in the area of Morro Bay that was responsible for placing the Nine Sisters.[53] Of course, the role of the turtle in supporting the Earth is a familiar one from Native lore. In this instance, the myth has not been elaborated upon; yet it is worth comparing it with René Guénon's description of the Ming T'ang or "Temple of Light" of the Chinese tradition that is attributed to Yü the Great: "He was inspired to this division into nine by the diagram called *Lo Chu* or 'Writing of the Lake' which according to legend was brought to him by a tortoise and in which the first nine numbers are arranged to form what is called a 'magic square;' in this way the Empire was made into an image of the Universe."[54] In both stories, a purposeful arrangement of the world is brought from the water by a turtle or tortoise. The first nine numbers represent a fullness of possibility in the Chinese example, and the numbering of the Morros at nine suggests that their landscape embodies a complete cosmos of California.

The most often repeated legend concerning the peaks is, not surprisingly, focused upon the eponymous Morro Rock specifically, and it is worth repeating here in detail. The following excerpt comes from the section "The Destruction of the Evil Monsters"[55] in J. Alden Mason's *Ethnography of the Salinan Indians*, published in 1912:

> Hawk and Raven then went hunting for more monsters, and sought a terrible two-headed

---

[52] See Randall Milliken and John R. Johnson, "An Ethnogeography of Salinan and Northern Chumash Communities – 1769 to 1810," Far Western Anthropological Research Group, March 2005.

[53] Ibid., page 134.

[54] *The Great Triad*, op. cit., pages 99-100.

[55] Cf. *Paths of the Western Sun*, volume I, page 56.

snake. When they approached, the snake…was sound asleep. "Now is the time! He is asleep!" said the Hawk to the Raven. They made some arrows from some reeds growing there and shot at the snake. First the Hawk hit him on one side and then the Raven hit the other. "Let us go before he gets up!" said the Hawk and they flew away. They travelled swiftly in the direction of Morro Rock on the seacoast, but the snake came swiftly after them, breaking down all the trees in his way. "Come on! Don't be afraid!" the Hawk who was in the lead kept calling to the Raven. Now the dust was close behind, but the Hawk said, "When we reach the Morro we'll be safe. The wind will help us there!" At last they reached the Morro, but in spite of the wind's efforts to foil him by breaking off pieces of rock, the snake encircled the rock and began to rise up…"What are we going to do now!" said the Raven. "Don't ask me that but just get ready!" replied the Hawk, as he pulled out a knife and began to hack away at the snake. Then the raven did the same on the other side of the rock, and the snake began to fall in pieces…[56]

In 1918, Mason provided a literal translation of the same legend,[57] and given its intended accuracy, details that have changed somewhat should not be overlooked. Hawk is now Prairie-Falcon, but surely this does not change the symbolism

---

[56] University of California Publications in American Archaeology and Ethnology, volume 10, number 4, pages 192-3.
[57] *The Language of the Salinan Indians,* University of California Publications in American Archaeology and Ethnology, volume 14, number 1, pages 112-4.

involved; after all, the ancient Greeks understood the falcon of Horus[58] to be the analogue of the hawk of Apollo. In this version, Raven asks Prairie-Falcon, "'Where is your power?'" and the reply is "'At the Morro; that is the last power.'"[59] Instead of striking the snake with simply a knife, Prairie-Falcon uses his "charm:" "With it he cut the snake into four pieces and killed him…And from these four pieces were formed the snakes of today." Finally the "old snake" says about these poisonous snakes: "'They shall live forever; I have died, but they will live.'"

If the symbolism of the raven may be understood to include a solar aspect, there is no denying the obvious solar significance of the hawk and prairie falcon alike.[60] As for their enemy, we have already encountered a two-headed serpent that seeks to eclipse the Sun in the lore surrounding the pseudoplanets. Moreover, despite the snake's dismemberment by Falcon, he speaks of immortality for his "pieces" in a manner that recalls the fate of Rahu and Ketu. The source of Falcon's power, Morro Rock, was recognized as a kind of fortress by the Spanish, and through the presence of the "encircling" serpent we are reminded that the dome of El Morro is also a circle, at least in its cross-section, and so partakes of the attributes of the Castle of Maidens. As for Gawain, the hero linked to this mythological motif, the etymology of his name is, remarkably enough, "falcon."

---

[58] The iconography of Horus reminds us that the animal-headed imagery of ancient Egypt may very well be related to the Native American stories of animals with human qualities.

[59] Raven's power is posited at two other hills near Cholam, and in a curious addition of his own, Mason identifies this region to be where the serpent also lived; however, since Cholam is eastwards of the missions for the Salinans, it is possible that what is essential here is the general direction offered by Mason.

[60] Like Apollo, Raven and Hawk are archers; and given the close relationship between raven and crow, it should not be overlooked that the crow was likewise sacred to Apollo.

The Last Power

With Morro Rock identified as the place of power for Falcon, its encircling serpent invites comparison with the ophidian "spirit of place" or genius loci[61] of Ancient Rome. Either singly or as a pair of serpents, the genius loci is often depicted in a coiled position around a stone altar (see page 41). In the Islamic tradition, an encircling serpent belongs to the otherworldly landscape of Mount Qāf, the cosmic mountain that surrounds this world that in turn is encircled by this great snake,[62] while Norse mythology offers its analogue in the world-encircling Midgard Serpent. Yet while these examples belong to the domain of the cosmos in its widest extent, we must not neglect the domain of the microcosm, especially since traditional doctrines already referred to have transmitted similar imagery that deserves a closer look. This imagery belongs to Tantrism and concerns the cosmic force of *Shakti* known as *Kundalinī*:

> The name *Kundalinī* signifies that it is represented as coiled about itself like a serpent, and indeed its most general manifestations are effected in the form of a spiral movement developing from a central point that is its 'pole.' The 'coiling' symbolizes a state of rest, that of a "static" energy from which all forms of activity proceed; in other words, all the more or less specialized vital forces constantly in action in the human individuality under its double

---

[61] Significantly, the word "genius" is the origin of the English word "genie," even though the latter refers to the jinn.

[62] In Arabic gematria, the name "Qāf" has the numerical value of 181; this is also the value of the word *maqam* that designates a spiritual "place" (cf. "The Place of Ivan Aguéli" in *Guardians of the Heart*, op. cit.). For a tale of the serpent of Qāf, see Michel Chodkiewicz, *Seal of the Saints: Prophethood and Sainthood in the Doctrine of Ibn `Arabi*, Cambridge: Islamic Texts Society, 1993, page 95.

> subtle and corporeal modality are only secondary aspects of that same *Shakti* which in itself, as *Kundalinī*, remains immobile in the "center-root"(*mūlādhāra*), as base and support of the whole manifestation. When "wide-awake" it uncoils and moves in an ascending direction…[63]

There are clear connections to be observed here, with even the "double" modality which Guénon describes recalling the two heads of the legendary snake. Moreover, the awakened serpent is rising in both examples. In the case of the *Kundalinī*, the serpentine power passes through the chakras of the human form, and three of the total number of chakras (which, as we have seen, varies) are characterized in further accord with the Salinan imagery. At the *ājñā* and *anāhata* chakras, as well as the *mūlādhāra* chakra, the Shakti is coiled around the symbolic lingas or "signs" of Shiva.[64] In Hinduism, when the linga of Shiva is represented, it takes the form of a stone, and as may be clearly seen on the opposite page, it bears a striking resemblance to the rock known as El Morro, especially since the serpent is an essential participant in its symbolism.

As for the designation "last power" that seems to refer to Morro Rock's position at the extremity of the Nine Sisters, we must admit that the Shakti at the *mūlādhāra* chakra might likewise be so designated, for while it serves as the starting point for spiritual realization, it is the lowermost in rank and so in a sense the last. Despite the discrepancy in the total number of chakras between different schema, all agree that there is at least one above the *ājñā* chakra but none below the *mūlādhāra*. It might further be offered that it is precisely at this chakra that the

---

[63] René Guénon, "*Kundalinī Yoga*," Studies in Hinduism, Hillsdale: Sophia Perennis, 2001, pages 21-2.
[64] Ibid. page 23.

Kundalinī remains for the majority of humanity, just as the poisonous snakes of Morro Rock have served as a tangible reminder of a continued presence there.

In *The New View Over Atlantis*, John Michell included the image at right of a genius loci, and offered the following caption: "The serpent spiraling up a pillar is a symbol of ancient mystical science, representing the fusion of earth energies with those of the cosmos and the stimulation

of spirit."[65] To provide evidence for his theories of "earth energies" Michell referred to the pioneering work of dowser Guy Underwood, and dowsers since the publication of Michell's seminal book have only elaborated upon his theories after their own manner. The very existence of "ley lines" has been dismissed by academics, but dowser Hamish Miller led an exploration of the Saint Michael Line across England that Michell himself discovered, and found that not one but *two* currents of energy flowed in mysterious harmony along this alignment.[66] The account of his team's exploration was called *The Sun and the Serpent*,[67] since the sinuous course of these lines of energy through the landscape suggested the form of serpents, in keeping with Michell's theories. More recently, David R. Cowan reported his observation that this earth energy proceeds specifically from volcanic plugs or lava necks, such as Castle Hill in Scotland;[68] and it will be recalled that the Nine Sisters are likewise lava necks, and indeed a most exceptional grouping of them. Certainly Native lore has preserved the notion of a two-fold serpentine presence there, in the form of a two-headed serpent.

Unfortunately, however, the meaning of "ley line" has been distorted by this emphasis on earth energies. Mapping the two currents of energy does not account for why their organic paths adhere to the rigors of a straight alignment. Simply put, the solution to this mystery relates to what the earth energies are

---

[65] *The New View Over Atlantis*, San Francisco: Harper & Row, 1983, page 199.

[66] Cf. *Sacred Geography and the Paths of the Sun*, op. cit., chapter 1. In microcosmic terms, the two currents of energy are embodied in the two principal *nadis* that wind around the axial *sushumnā* and cross at the various chakras (cf. ibid., page 47).

[67] Paul Broadhurst and Hamish Miller, *The Sun and the Serpent*, Launceston: Pendragon Press, 1989.

[68] Cf. Cowan with Anne C. Silk, *Ley Lines of the U.K. and U.S.A.*, Kempton: Adventures Unlimited Press, 2013.

meant to be fused with according to the above quote, namely "those of the cosmos." I attempted to clarify this matter for Europe in my *Sacred Geography and the Paths of Sun*, since despite its title, *The Sun and the Serpent* fails to address the Sun's privileged position in this cosmic fusion. In California, El Morro is not the "place of power" for the two-headed serpent of the earth, after all, but for the falcon, the bird of the Sun.

○

A puerile interpretation of the story of Falcon and Raven at Morro Rock would only take from it an explanation of how rattlesnakes came to be at that place. To imagine that the rattlesnakes are the inspiration for the legendary serpent encircling El Morro reverses the traditional understanding of the latter being the ontological source of the former. The rattlesnakes are rather proof of the veracity of the legend. Comparable testimony is provided by the eyries of falcons, specifically of Peregrine Falcons, that are still present at Falcon's place of power. While ornithological classifications may not be consistent with the legend, or even be consistent among its different versions, as we have seen, the symbolism clearly is. The survival of the falcons at Morro Rock is despite the devastation inflicted upon them through the tyrannical use of pesticides in the 20th century. At present, bird populations seem to be recovering, at least in California, and as a protective measure the trail by which people had formerly ascended El Morro has been closed to the public. Unfortunately, the very policy designed to heal the place has been used to disrupt its traditional purpose.

A *Los Angeles Times* article from 2002, "Messy Affair Plays Out Atop a Famed Rock,"[69] describes John Burch's

---

[69] Dated 7 February, in the "Living" section.

struggles to maintain practices he inherited from his Salinan ancestors. Morro Rock is presented in the article as "where the Falcon of ancient legend killed the serpent Teleekatapelta." Burch's responsibility is to ascend the sacred height and perform a vigil through the night. The vigil involved sitting upon a "throne," although this word is surely meant to convey the dignity associated with a traditional stone arrangement rather than the appearance of the seat itself.[70] The timing for the ritual is "on dates prescribed by the heavens," and these dates are specifically associated with the solstices and equinoxes of the Sun, although only the solstices are mentioned as being observed. Despite the ban on climbing the rock, Burch was apparently able to procure a permit to do so on religious grounds, especially since his conduct was acknowledged to be far less disturbing to bird populations than the work of biologists. However, Chumash representatives insist that the "sacred shrine" of Morro Rock is "Chumash territory" and oppose Burch's fulfilment of Salinan sacred duty. While admitting that they too had in former times climbed the lava neck for ritual purposes, the Chumash maintain that no one should any longer be allowed because of the threat to the falcons. The objectivity of the Chumash tribal lawyer quoted in the article, however, is undermined by her leadership of a local chapter of the Sierra Club.

---

[70] I encountered a similar description of stone "thrones" in Northern Oregon upon Mount Angel, the ancient "Mount of Communion." In this case, confusion has resulted from the use of that term, in particular since the Benedictines now occupying the site – and still using it for "Communion" – seemed to be unaware of the stone seats of Native tradition that are known by the Yuroks of Northern California as *tsektsel* (cf. Haynal, Patrick M., "The Influence of Sacred Rock Cairns and Prayer Seats on Modern Klamath and Modoc Religion and World View," *Journal of California and Great Basin Anthropology*, 22(2), University of California Merced, 2000).

This is indeed an affair made "messy" by politics. It is all too clear that the threat to the falcons was never the practice of ancient tradition, but rather the excesses of secular science. More than this, to ascend Morro Rock is to honor the example of Falcon. The view that the peak should be left for the animals is not a traditional one; after all, the Salinan story belongs to the time "when all the animals were men"[71] anyway. The Chumash lawyer offers that "there are many places you can hold ceremonies," which ignores what Burch describes as a "spiritual door" that opens during the deliberately timed rituals upon El Morro's summit. Strictly speaking, and despite the modern usage of the words, the public performance of ceremonies is not the same as a ritual.[72]

It should be unnecessary to insist upon the importance of place in ritual, but it is nevertheless instructive to recall a comparable example from volume I of *Paths of the Western Sun*. As I mentioned in *Ancient Secrets of the Rogue Valley*, the Native "Salmon Ceremony" has in recent years returned to the Rogue River through the efforts of Agnes Baker Pilgrim. Previously, she had carried out the ceremony alongside another river in the same region. The importance of the Rogue River location was centered in the "Story Chair" where Pilgrim's ancestors had sat, and this stone structure could easily be called a "throne." It was from this seat that the ritual elements of the Salmon Ceremony were traditionally accomplished. Moreover, only by navigating the waterfalls surrounding it could this ritual seat be reached, and this may be compared to the challenge of ascending Morro Rock. Unlike the social ceremony, the ritual is tied to a specific site; and while it would be more convenient not to bother with

---

[71] Mason 1912, page 192.

[72] To be clear, the Chumash especially are known to have observed solstice rituals; see for example T. Hudson et al., "Solstice Observers and Observatories in Native California," *Journal of California and Great Basin Anthropology*, volume 1, number 1, Malki Museum, summer 1979.

the challenge of reaching the sacred seat, that is where the qualified human representative is in view of the journeying salmon. Is it not conceivable that the qualified human being atop Morro Rock must likewise sit in view of the falcons for the ritual to be properly accomplished?[73]

Following the appearance of the news report, Angela Howard Dillon prepared a more detailed study of the controversy surrounding Morro Rock as an academic project. She reports on attempts to discredit John Burch through insubstantial suspicions that he only sought worldly gain by asserting the Salinan claim on land to be developed for a local electrical power station. Clearer insight into Burch's activities, and the purpose of the Salinan ritual, was fortunately gleaned from his sister Patti:

> On the summer solstice, when the sun was at its furthest point north, the Salinans climbed Morro Rock to pray for the sun to return. They feared that, without their prayers, the sun would disappear in the distance and might never return. They also prayed for safe passage to the next world for loved ones that had passed on. Patti mentioned that the rocks (referring to the series of nine volcanic plugs that stretch from San Luis Obispo into the Pacific) were "magnetic" but was "not sure if that plays into anything." When Patti's mother was a girl, Morro Rock was completely surrounded by water. Kids used to take rowboats out to the rock but they were unable to land because of

---

[73] Despite there being no legal obstacle to reaching the Rogue River's Story Chair, the late Agnes Baker Pilgrim was the last authorized person to sit in the chair over a decade ago now, and tribal politics are not absent from this situation either.

hundreds of little black rattlesnakes that inhabited it. The Salinans believed that all rattlesnakes originated from those on Morro Rock.

The association of the summer solstice with the fate of souls is a familiar one in Native tradition, and I have in previous writings examined a wealth of evidence relating to this theme provided by the Achumawi of Northern California. I have further insisted upon the equivalence between this theme and the beliefs of the ancient Pythagoreans. In multiple articles, René Guénon has clarified the Pythagorean doctrine of the solstices as doors or gates for souls.[74] More generally, Pythagoras seems to have transmitted teachings from an even more ancient past, as he seems to have done with his most famous teaching, the so-called "Pythagorean Theorem," that has been found in monuments like Stonehenge that predate the Greeks. For his followers, Pythagoras was the heir of Apollo himself, perhaps even his son, and the primordial character of the Apollonian tradition is expressed through the god's affiliation with the Hyperboreans of the Golden Age. The primordiality of Pythagorean wisdom is confirmed by the Islamic tradition that regards him to be a student of Hermes, or rather the second form of the Thrice-Great Hermes, since the knowledge of Hermes is traced in Islam to the time before the Flood. In any case, if Pythagoreanism is in accord with Native tradition, there is no reason to dismiss it as coincidence; it is far more reasonable to suspect the presence of the Primordial Tradition.

In *Sacred Geography and the Paths of the Sun*, I presented the evidence for the Pythagoreans being involved in an alignment through Europe only recently discovered and referred to as the "Axis of Saint Michael and of Apollo." From

---

[74] See for example "The Solstitial Gates" and "The Symbolism of the Zodiac Among the Pythagoreans" in *Symbols of Sacred Science* (op. cit.).

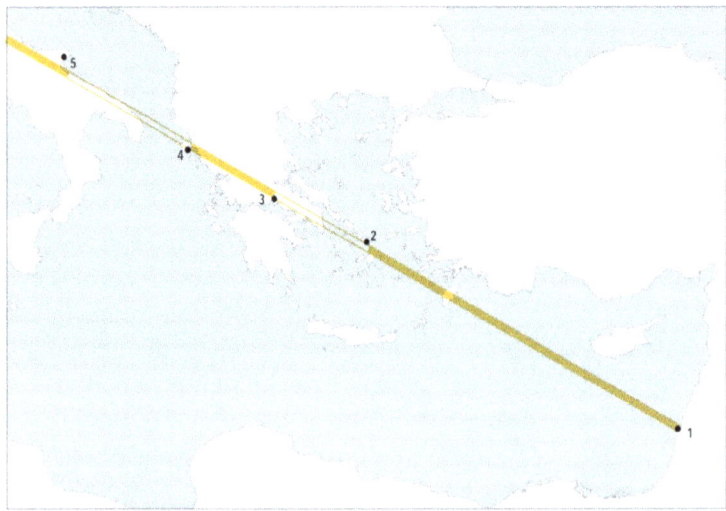

Mount Carmel in the Holy Land, the azimuth of the summer solstice sunset leads to the Temple of Apollo in Delphi through other Apollonian shrines; and Pythagoras himself is known to have visited both Mount Carmel (point 1 in the above map) and Delphi (point 3). At the temple in Delphi, there is evidence that this solstitial alignment was in some measure recognized and symbolized by the octopus and dolphin. Specifically, the octopus is the emblem of the summer solstice and the dolphin the emblem of the winter solstice, and it is worth observing that both solstices are relevant here. Besides the relationship of the landscape alignment to the summer solstice azimuth, the same alignment looking to the southeast corresponds to the azimuth of the winter solstice sunrise.

Returning to the controversy at Morro Rock, it will be recalled that the timing of the Salinan ritual supposedly belongs to both solstices. There is another curious comparison to be made between the Salinan legend of the serpent Teleekatapelta and the lore of Delphi, since Apollo established his temple there through the defeat of the monstrous serpent Python. Dillon's

The Last Power

Apollo Vanquishing the Serpent Python
Gustave Moreau, c. 1885

Salinan source offers that the Nine Sisters are magnetic, which recalls the dowsing for electromagnetic lines of force along the Saint Michael Line in Britain. In fact, this approach was subsequently applied to the Axis of Saint Michel and of Apollo, with comparable observations made concerning two meandering lines of force that nevertheless adhered to a straight trajectory.[75] In the case of the Nine Sisters, the special nature of their linear arrangement is easily acknowledged; what has never until now been observed is that this arrangement essentially corresponds to the azimuths of the solstices. From San Luis Obispo, the line of lava necks follows the summer solstice sunset, whereas from Morro Rock the alignment back to the southeast aligns with the sunrise azimuth on the winter solstice.[76]

It is common knowledge that Stonehenge in England is oriented to the summer solstice sunrise, and that it has served as a mortuary monument; but despite the incorporation of "Pythagorean" geometry, there has been a failure to consider the relevance of Pythagorean doctrine concerning the fate of souls. In California we are far further from the lands visited by Pythagoras, yet the similarities between the Apollonian tradition he represented and the rituals of Morro Rock are remarkably precise. From the "throne" atop El Morro, the summer sunset alignment before the night vigil would be apparent, as would that of the winter solstice sunrise after the vigil. Beyond this, the "spiritual door" mentioned by John Burch

---

[75] This journey along the Axis of Saint Michael and of Apollo was recounted by Broadhurst and Miller in *The Dance of the Dragon* (Launceston: Pendragon Press, 2000).

[76] Since the solstices mark the northern and southern limits of the Sun's movement, they represent the north-south axis of the year in contrast to the obvious east-west domain of the equinoxes, as I have mentioned in volume I of *Paths of the Western Sun* (page 73); for this reason, it is worth taking note of the axial presentation of the massive sandspit due south of Morro Rock.

The Last Power

is surely analogous to the zodiacal doors of the Pythagoreans. According to that doctrine, the spiritual door is the *janua coeli* or "Door of Heaven" that is open to the elect only on the winter solstice; the summer solstice offers the *janua inferni* or "Door of the Underworld," and it was understood to function as the way in and out of this world for the generality of souls. The name of the latter has been perpetuated by Dante's "Inferno," since the Underworld Door involved psychic possibilities other than heavenly; for the Pythagoreans as for the Salinans, prayers during the summer solstice would no doubt help ensure "safe passage to the next world for loved ones that had passed on."

In this context, the two-headed snake clearly appears as another formulation of the "Guardian of the Sundoor."[77] The griffin was mentioned above in connection with this mythological motif, and its dual composition may easily be compared with the two heads of the serpent. The guardians are usually ophidian and often paired,[78] and must be overcome by solar heroes who thereby ensure safe passage for the souls who follow them. The slaying of Python by Apollo may have been necessary, yet a mysterious continuity at the doorways of Delphi is suggested by the title "Pythia" for Apollo's representative.

No doubt the preservation of falcons is an important aspect of sustaining the sacred landscape of the Nine Sisters in California. Yet following the legendary victory of Falcon and Raven, the sacred purpose of the Morro fortress was fulfilled only through the vigilance of "gatekeepers."

---

[77] See Coomaraswamy, op. cit.

[78] Cf. the Talisman Gate in Baghdad, the traditional seat of the Caliph, pictured on page 54 of *Mysteries of Dune*; its iconography recalls Hercules' vanquishing of the serpents in his crib, with the crib being associated with entering this world. This year in England, an important discovery was made on the summer solstice at the Long Man of Wilmington, proving that despite the long-held opinion of "ley hunters," the effigy is depicted holding the jambs of the Sundoor (see my "Recognizing the Long Man of Wilmington").

A "mystery wall" along El Camino Real
Highway 101 follows the Spanish route through a natural gap into San Luis Obispo.

4

An Ancient Science

The conformity of a landscape with solstitial azimuths demonstrates a correspondence of "earth energies with those of the cosmos," and allows for their "fusion," at least potentially.[79] If lava necks are indeed points of emanation for earth energies, as dowsing indicates, then the alignment of the Nine Sisters of California is even more exceptional. Given that no artificial modification may be supposed in the raising of these lava necks, we should not expect artificial precision in the geometry of their alignment. As the map on page 54 shows, the sequence of the Nine Sisters seems very akin to the undulating course of the natural energies described by dowsers. The solstitial azimuth running through Morro Rock connects it precisely with the distant Cerro San Luis; the other peaks are displaced immediately to the north of this line, with the terminal Islay Hill just to the south. Here it is possible to distinguish the straightness of the solar azimuth from the wave-like contours of the earth energies that nevertheless appear bound to it. This sinusoidal characteristic recalls the vibrations of a linear string

---

[79] For other American examples of "topographical peculiarities" in the science of sacred geography, see chapter 5 of *Paths of the Western Sun*, volume I.

The Nine Sisters of California

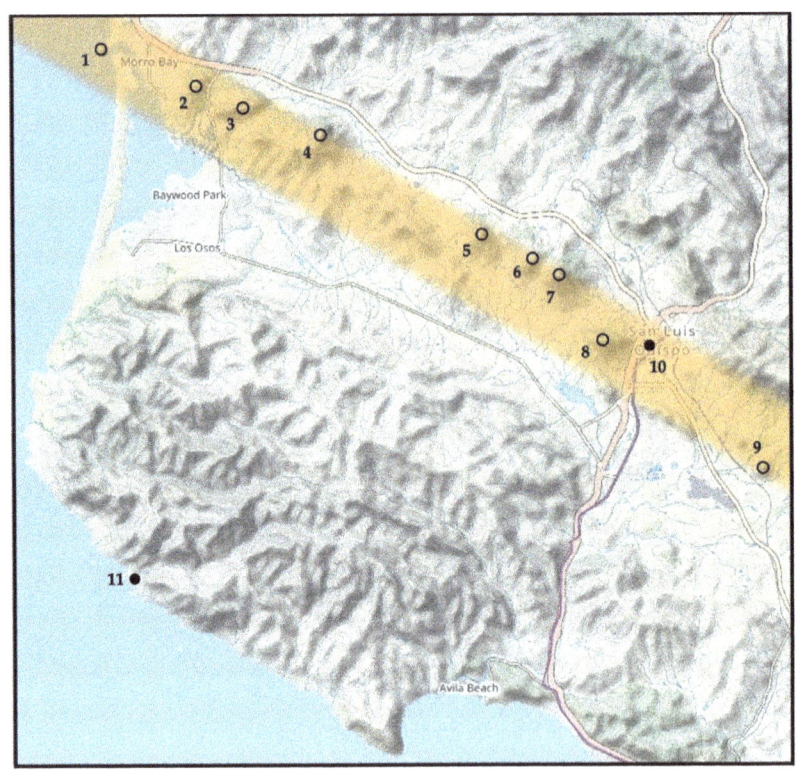

Solstitial Alignment of the Nine Sisters

1. Morro Rock
2. Black Hill
3. Cerro Cabrillo
4. Hollister Peak
5. Cerro Romauldo
6. Chumash Peak
7. Bishop Peak
8. Cerro San Luis Obispo
9. Islay Hill
10. Mission San Luis Obispo de Tolosa
11. Diablo Canyon

or chord, an observation of particular relevance to the Pythagorean emphasis on sound for understanding the composition of the cosmos. If the azimuth line is widened to include all Nine Sisters, we are able to conceptualize an axial corridor or pathway rather than a line. The resulting pathway may, since it corresponds to a solar azimuth, be properly identified as a "Path of the Sun."

Where Paths of the Sun follow azimuths of the solstices, as is the case here, the corresponding alignments are synonymous with the "paths of the dead," in keeping with the doctrine of the solstitial doors.[80] In my effort to provide some preliminary comments on the so-called 'mystery walls" that remain so widespread upon the American landscape,[81] I observed that they are often concentrated in conjunction with the "paths of the dead" of Native tradition. It is therefore reasonable to expect in the environs of the Nine Sisters the presence of those mysterious linear cairns that are also known as the "East Bay Walls;" and in fact, this particular area seems to have the greatest concentration of these ancient cairns than anywhere south of the East Bay, at least within the boundaries of our "island" of California. As always when evaluating surviving cairns as part of a sacred landscape, it is important to consider the role of modern development in damaging them, as well as of historical modification for mundane purposes, especially ranching. In many cases these cairn networks must therefore be considered to be incomplete, yet this fact does not essentially change one of their fundamental attributes, namely their discontinuity.

The most extensive network appears to be located upon a ridge to the north of Morro Rock, and despite the distance

---

[80] It is not by accident that churches dedicated specifically to Saint Michael, the psychopomp of Christendom, were built along the solstitial Path of the Sun through Europe.

[81] "Some Remarks on the 'Mystery Walls,'" *Guardians of the Heart*.

separating them, there is reason to suspect that this network is not unrelated to El Morro.[82] As for the chain of lava necks, it is important to understand that it is bordered by valleys that are more or less parallel with it, and that flanking the valleys to the north and south are further ridges of hills. To the north of the Chorro Valley, there are several concentrations of linear cairn networks, while south of the Los Osos Valley, the cairns seem to be focused in a single area. Between the valleys, and therefore along the axis of the chain of peaks, there are also linear cairns, but they do not seem to be found upon the Nine Sisters themselves. As may be seen from the map on page 54, the nine peaks appear divided into two groups of four, with the easternmost Islay Hill standing somewhat apart. The linear cairns are found upon lesser hills between the two main groups.

One such hill warrants our attention, if only because its position is uniquely in line with the solstitial azimuth extending from Cerro San Luis to Morro Rock.[83] Linear cairns are found upon its entire length, and we needn't be concerned that wire ranch fencing extends beyond the end of the stone "walls" in a typical display of repurposing. The antecedence of the stone

---

[82] With mystery walls elsewhere being associated with serpentine symbolism (see "Some Remarks on the 'Mystery Walls,'" op. cit., page 50), it is worth noting the possible relationship between the Salinan legend of the dismembered serpent and the discontinuous linear cairns in the vicinity.

[83] Immediately below this hill and overlooking Chorro Creek is an enormous monolith, and one can only wonder what significance this site may have had before becoming a historic ranch. For what it's worth, this monolith represents the midpoint between the two groups of four lava necks mentioned above (that is, all the peaks except for Islay Hill that is set apart); and the midpoint of a vibrating chord represents a still point or node that, when held, raises the tone of the chord by an octave. Again, the choice of which hills to include among the Nine Sisters is somewhat arbitrary, and excluding Islay Hill would also narrow the solar corridor substantially.

Mystery wall and lava neck

constructions is borne out by a short, isolated remnant below the hill that was not incorporated into the ranch fence. Near the summit of the hill it is clear that there are actually three distinct walls that diverge from a single point, with their respective positions balanced in a manner that suggests a three-fold division of the surroundings.

One wall extends along the length of the hill below the summit and descends gradually towards the Chorro Valley. Another section extends to the summit and to the edge of the Los Osos Valley but is only a few feet in length. Most noteworthy is the course of the remaining wall, since it descends the steep slope of the hill in perfect alignment with the summit of the nearest of the Nine Sisters (see previous page). These observations are especially worthwhile because meeting places of three walls, as well as alignments between walls and lava necks, are observable elsewhere within the modern state of California. If a lava neck that is "magnetic" for the Salinans is indeed a source of dowsable energy, it might be possible to determine whether the cairn that is oriented towards it somehow relates to this energy. Needless to say, such notions will never be considered by archaeologists who fail to even recognize the existence of the ancient cairns.

It is therefore worth acknowledging a recent archaeological survey undertaken for the city of San Luis Obispo at the historic Froom Ranch.[84] The archaeologists took the unusual position of admitting that four "linear rock wall features" were most likely of Native construction. Of course, these features are exceptionally low and would therefore be of no use as walls to dairy farmers, and as is the case with mystery walls elsewhere, they do not enclose anything. What is more, these alignments attracted special consideration due to the

---

[84] The archaeologists' findings were included in a draft of the "Froom Ranch Specific Plan" made available online by the city of San Luis Obispo.

An Ancient Science

rather unusual fact that they appear to be paired.[85] Obviously the survey's unusual position was made safer by the ample evidence of Native tradition at the site. This evidence includes a number of holed stones, but here the report unfortunately repeats the erroneous notion that such holes in California were for grinding acorns.

The term "mortar" connotes function and so it is not used here, since it is far from understood what these cup marks signify. They are found worldwide, and in evidence at the earliest of temples such as Göbekli Tepe. Their presence is a widespread characteristic of the island of California as we have defined it, but they are also concentrated along the western foothills of the Sierras, that is, on the opposite side of the ancient waters that isolated California. Indeed, the greatest concentration anywhere of such holes upon a single rock is found at Indian Grinding Rock State Park, where petroglyphs embellish this tableau of over a thousand holes. Regardless of where they are found, they are perfectly useless in the processing of acorns. On the other hand, their receptivity in relation to the sky make them repositories for rain, the most tangible symbol of heavenly influence, although their usefulness in this regard depends upon diligence in keeping them clean. Wherever they are found, it is reasonable to suppose that their presence marks a location of sacred importance and not a food factory; for despite the materialistic bias of modern science that presumes only subsistence would necessitate the creation of these holes, it is rather the heavenly that mattered most to all the traditional worlds.[86]

With acorns having no value to modern people, attributing these markings to acorn processing ensures that they

---

[85] Parallel alignments are best exemplified in the so-called "reaves" of Dartmoor in Britain.
[86] Cf. the marking at the Station of Abraham and the Divine injunction to worship there in *The Red and the White*, chapter 6.

are accorded little attention; yet holed stones have been reported in several locations among the Nine Sisters, in particular below Bishop Peak and between Black Hill and Cerro Cabrillo. An especially large collection of cupped stones distinguishes a site above Churro Creek midway along the chain of peaks. No doubt this sacred site was a key location to ancient people, and it has thankfully been spared the ravages of modern development. Although the focus of this site seems to be more immediate than the Nine Sisters themselves, the complex is more centered along the axial corridor than the wall networks of the Chorro Valley, and two of the peaks are in plain sight of the holed stones (see facing page).

The Chinese tradition of the "Writing of the Lake" was mentioned in the last chapter, and the traditional diagram shows how this "writing" upon the back of the cosmic tortoise involved a precise arrangement of points. Without insisting on an exact equivalence, it is worth observing that the holed stones are quite literally an arrangement of points upon the earth. This

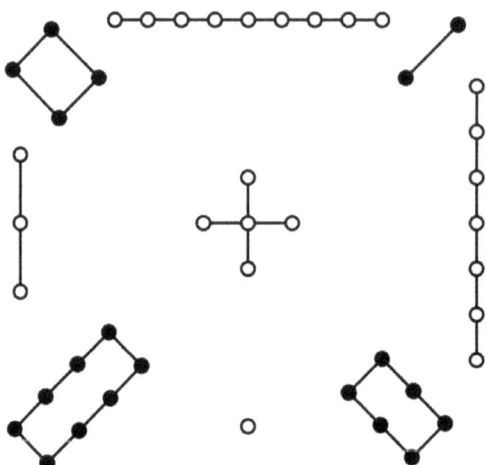

The Writing of the Lake

An Ancient Science

Peaks and repositories

Chinese diagram is of essential importance to feng-shui, a cosmological science involving the cultivation of beneficial energies in the landscape. John Michell maintained that it was this science that was the inspiration for the wall network known as the Great Wall of China, even if this network had been repurposed for military defense by the Middle Ages.[87] As I have acknowledged elsewhere, mysterious walls are found worldwide, as are the holed stones,[88] but what makes the American landscape so special is that such signs of an ancient cosmological science comparable to the foundations of feng-shui are still to be found upon it. Given the contemporary ignorance of these signs, it is easily assumed that ancient science meant nothing to the Spanish conquerors of California either. Evidence is only now coming to light that, quite unexpectedly, dispels this assumption.

---

[87] Cf. John Michell, *The Earth Spirit: Its Ways, Shrines and Mysteries*, Singapore: Thames and Hudson, 1989, page 16.

[88] For more on cupped stones, see *The Red and the White* (chapter 6) and *Arthurian Matters of Britain: Celtic-Christian-Islamic* (forthcoming from Temple of Justice Books, section on "The Rain Stone").

5

The Church with Two Naves

The small city of San Luis Obispo is nestled at the base of Cerro San Luis of the Nine Sisters, the peak in perfect solstitial alignment with Morro Rock. The city is named for its mission, which like so many of the California missions was named for a saint of the Franciscan Order, in this case San Luis Obispo de Tolosa, or Saint Louis, Bishop of Toulouse. The mission was built upon a rise above a principal watercourse, and the reasons for selecting this site for the mission would no doubt have included its utility in influencing the local Native population. Thereafter, the deliberate position of the mission church apparently determined the layout of the town, which is hardly strange, but the street grid of downtown San Luis Obispo is strangely out of keeping with the cardinal directions, at least before the construction of outlying roads that are. Even more strangely, the mission does not conform to the direction we should expect a Catholic church to face. The very meaning of the word "orientation" is inseparable from the custom of aligning a church towards the east, yet the mission church at San Luis Obispo is turned to the northwest.

The proper alignment of a Catholic church is clear from a commentary by the French bishop William Durandus in the 13th century, which is worth quoting here if only for the fact that

Saint Louis of Toulouse was likewise a French bishop of the 13th century:

> The foundation must be so contrived, as that the Head of the Church may point due East; that is, to the point of the heavens, wherein the sun ariseth at the equinox; to signify, that the Church Militant must behave herself with moderation, both in prosperity and adversity: and not towards that point where the sun ariseth at the solstices, which is the practice of some.[89]

That the "head" of Mission San Luis Obispo is turned away from the east must therefore be recognized as being contrary to established tradition; yet among the Spanish missions such an orientation turns out to be far from exceptional. The Carmel Mission, the headquarters of all the missions of Alta California between 1797 and 1833, is positioned so that its head is directed southwest to the Pacific Ocean. To the south of San Luis Obispo and likewise linked to the Chumash, the mission church of Santa Barbara is turned to the northwest, while the two missions associated with the Salinans, those of San Antonio de Padua and San Miguel, both face northwest, albeit in varying degrees. Without digressing into a complete inventory,[90] there is ample evidence of a particular but unorthodox architectural agenda at work. It had formerly been assumed that practical lighting

---

[89] J.M. Neale and B. Webb, *The Symbolism of Churches and Church Ornaments: A Translation of the First Book of the Rationale Divinorum Officiorum Written by William Durandus*, Leeds: T.W. Green, 1843, pages 21-2.

[90] It is worth noting the case of Mission Santa Clara as well, since it reportedly faced east before a 19th century reconstruction literally flipped its position on its plaza to face west.

considerations determined the unusual and varied orientations of the mission churches, as if lighting had never been a concern for Medieval Christendom. However, the recent discoveries of a Catholic academic, Rubén G. Mendoza, have revealed the nature of the missionaries' agenda.

Mendoza has established that at least for the majority of the Alta California missions, the builders arranged for "solar illuminations" to occur through precise architectural planning in subtle harmony with the Sun's path in the sky. On a chosen day, a ray of light would be directed through a window or door towards the tabernacle of the church to illuminate Catholic iconography specific to that day. The aim of presenting these illuminations to worshippers seems to account for the break with Catholic tradition, since witnesses would need to be turned away from the source of light. What is of further interest here is that it was more often than not a solstitial Sun that would be the source of light. At the Carmel Mission, for example, the church is aligned precisely with the summer solstice sunrise in order to receive its light; its axis therefore corresponds exactly to that azimuth. Mendoza has also studied in depth the solstice sunrise illuminations of the mission church of San Juan Bautista.[91] Since the worshippers in the mission churches were predominantly Native, the solstices may very well have been chosen to embellish rather than destroy the Native understanding, and Mendoza suspects that a Native influence may even have been involved in the setting up of these illuminations.[92]

Despite Durandus' emphasis on the equinox and disdain for solstitial symbolism, Roman Catholicism nevertheless inherited a more ancient understanding of the winter solstice akin to that of the Pythagoreans. It is generally

---

[91] Rubén Mendoza, "Sacrament of the Sun: Eschatological Architecture and Solar Geometry in a California Mission," *Boletín: The Journal of the California Mission Studies Association*, volume 22, number 1, spring 2005.
[92] Ibid., page 108.

admitted that the observance of Jesus' birth on 25 December was "a deliberate attempt to replace the pagan feast of the Invincible Sun with the true Sun of Justice."[93] Mendoza supports the view that this formulation of *Christo-Helios* became the distinctive focus of Native Christianity, to the extent that the "sunburst monstrance" that emerges among the mendicant orders in the Americas may be seen as a synthesis of Roman Catholic and Native imagery.[94] Whereas the Sun's rebirth at the time of the winter solstice was traditionally associated with the *janua coeli* or "Door of Heaven," Roman Christianity more generally adopted this symbolism for its churches: "Awesome is this place: here is the house of God and the gate of Heaven."[95] With solar illuminations relating to the winter solstice, the mission churches therefore represent a convergence of these two notions, respectively temporal and spatial, of the "Door of Heaven."

Despite having its main door oriented to the southeast, the axis of the church of San Luis Obispo does not correspond to the azimuth of the winter solstice sunrise. Instead, the church is positioned so that its northeastern side faces the *summer* solstice sunrise. The axis of the church is therefore exactly perpendicular to that azimuth, although the symbolic crossing of the church or transept must then necessarily correspond to it. Such an alignment is likewise demonstrated at Mission San Antonio de Padua. In San Luis Obispo, it is worth observing that this

---

[93] Ibid., page 104.

[94] Ibid., page 102. It is worth pointing out that while the Roman festival of the Invincible Sun was linked to the figure of Apollo, Apollo is properly not the god of the Sun (Helios) but of light; and it is significant that ancient depictions of Apollo as a shepherd provided models for the earliest anthropomorphic images of Jesus Christ. Since Apollo is more than Helios, we should avoid reducing solar symbolism to "Sun worship," and the same care should be taken with Native doctrines that are so comparable to those of the Apollonian tradition.

[95] *Roman Missal*.

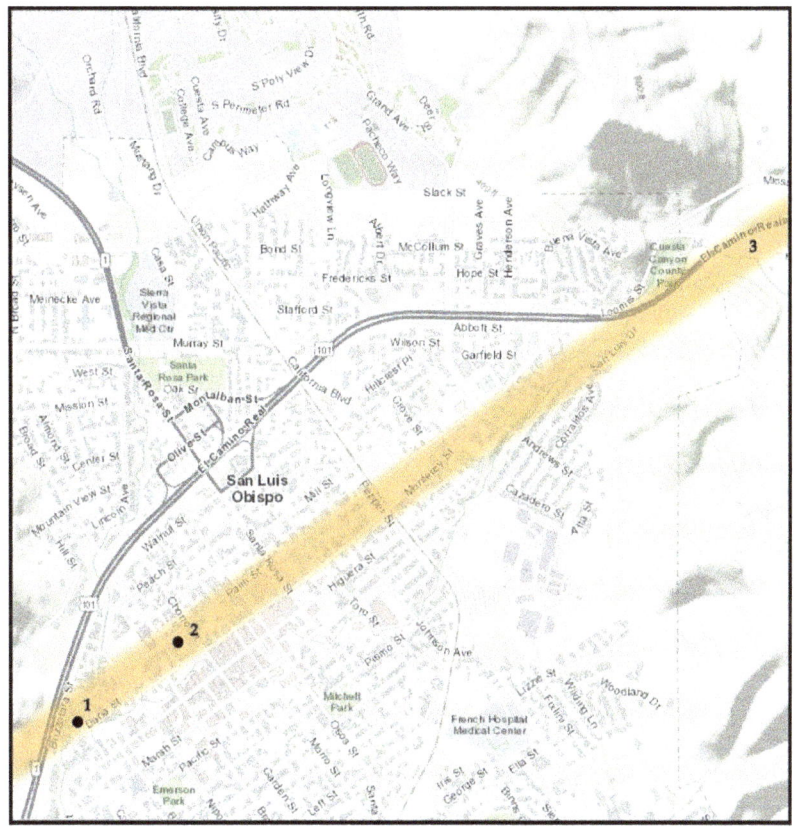

***Solstitial Axis of San Luis Obispo*[96]**

1 Original mission location (projected)
2 Mission San Luis Obispo de Tolosa
3 Natural opening into San Luis Obispo

---

[96] While not apparent on this map, the axis of the church is actually closer to the solstitial azimuth than the street grid that developed from it.

solstitial azimuth reaches the mission through a natural gap in the hills to the northeast, and this gap was in fact the route chosen for El Camino Real, no doubt in accordance with an older path. The importance of this gap is no doubt indicated by a concentration of mystery walls in the vicinity (see page 52), one of several mentioned previously as being positioned north of the Nine Sisters. The natural feature would almost certainly have been a consideration in choosing the specific site for the mission.

 We must acknowledge, however, that the mission's present location was not the place selected by Father Junipero Serra for its first mass in 1772. The first church was reportedly at the confluence of two creeks, and so the nearby confluence of San Luis Creek and Brizziolari Creek has been identified as the mission's original location. As the map shows, the azimuth of the summer solstice sunrise that passes through the present mission in fact extends to this original location, and even more remarkably, this original site is actually more in line with the sunset azimuth passing through Cerro San Luis and Morro Rock. Be that as it may, both mission locations accommodate these astronomical considerations, although the shifting of the mission to higher ground would necessarily have improved the effect of the solstice sunrise through the nearby gap.

 The clearest testimony of the importance of this sunrise dimension is expressed in the present layout of the mission church, for Mission San Luis Obispo is unique in having a L-shaped floorplan. Now, it is not unusual for churches since the Middle Ages to be constructed around two axes that cross, with the principle axis represented by the nave of the church and the other by the transept. Where the two axes meet is called the crossing, while the sanctuary is properly beyond the crossing at the far end of the nave. The layout of the mission church, however, suggests rather two naves oriented at right angles to each other, since they meet rather at the sanctuary of the church; as a result, pews are able to be arranged along both axes. The secondary nave, then, represents the solstitial axis of Mission

The Church with Two Naves

The second nave, or annex, of Mission San Luis Obispo (above), looking towards the sanctuary

The end of the annex (right) directed towards the summer solstice sunrise

San Luis Obispo. At present, there is no door open to the sunrise direction, but rather a single window placed high in the wall that would allow the light of the solstice Sun to shine upon the far wall of the sanctuary, with the pews of the church appropriately facing that direction (see previous page).

It is currently maintained that the statue of Saint Louis of Toulouse is positioned in the middle of this far wall in accordance with modern convention: "In other missions, the patron saint of the church is often found above the altar, but in a modern parish the Crucifix holds this revered position."[97] However, the floor plan of Mission San Luis Obispo is unlike any other, and it is not known where the original statue of Saint Louis was located. In any case, its present placement "high on

the wall" is perfectly suited to be illuminated by the summer solstice sunrise. What is more, the statue is positioned alongside a window that, because of the solstitial alignment of the secondary nave, directly transmit the rays of the winter solstice sunset (at left).

Yet it would seem that this secondary nave was not part of the church's original plan at all: "The 'L' wing, or annex, of the church dates from the American era, around 1893, and was extended in 1947," that is, long after the Franciscans had left the mission. The curious decision to expand the mission – on two occasions – is rather incongruous in terms of demographics and has no obvious precedent in California. Very likely, a plan to extend the church along the solstitial axis

---

[97] Quotations are from "Mission San Luis Obispo de Tolosa: A Self Guided Tour," a pamphlet available in the mission gift shop.

already existed before 1893 but historical circumstances delayed its realization. Regardless, a "solar illumination" does not require an "annex" anyway but only an opening, as well as a target for the rays of the Sun. Still, just as the present mission site represents an extension of sorts from its original location along the solstitial azimuth, so too did the extensions of the American era proceed along that same axis. When looking in vain for a mundane explanation, it should not be forgotten that the church remained under the spiritual direction, or patronage, of a Franciscan saint, despite the absence of the padres.

o

Mendoza places the solar illuminations of the California missions within the context of an overall architectural plan that anticipates the Heavenly Jerusalem. Millenarian expectations were defined for the Franciscans of the New World by the writings of Fray Jerónimo de Mendieta (1525-1604): "Mendieta's prophetic mysticism emphasized the role of Spain, particularly Spanish Franciscans, in establishing the *christianorum imperium* or universal monarchy…In his view, the Spanish crown and its military and religious forces would ultimately serve as the gatekeepers of the impending apocalypse foretold in the Book of Revelations."[98] Mendoza mentions the "twin rallying cries" of these expectations: "*Santiago Matamoros* (Santiago the Killer of Moors)" and "*Santiago Mataindios* (Santiago the Killer of Indians)." Santiago, of course, is Saint James of Compostela, the patron saint of Spain; and though the latter formula was employed especially in Latin America, there is a curious relevance to both of these "twin cries" in the context of San Luis Obispo. After all, the Nine Sisters are also the Morros, and we

---

[98] Mendoza, op. cit., page 89.

have already examined the Crusading context of this terminology.

By virtue of its location among the Morros, the mission church of San Luis Obispo relates to the summer solstice sunset, even though its more immediate focus is towards the summer solstice sunrise. At the same time, we have seen that the alignment of lava necks relates also to the midwinter sunrise. In a comparable manner, the church axis corresponding to midsummer sunrise must also relate to the azimuth of the midwinter sunset, and we have noted the specific inclusion of a window to that direction in the church's design. Extending this winter solstice azimuth beyond San Luis Obispo may be abstract, since it does not apparently correspond to the geography,[99] but it is surely not without meaning that this alignment extends to the neighboring community of Avila Beach; after all, despite the secular circumstances of its naming, Avila Beach necessarily evokes Santa Teresa, from whom the name of Ávila is inseparable.[100] In the 16th century, the recently canonized Santa Teresa was enormously popular, and very nearly replaced Saint James as the patron saint of Spain. Leaving aside the rather dubious character of the claims of the shrine in Compostela,[101] it would be difficult to imagine a more profound contrast between the two representatives of Spanish sainthood. Whereas Matamoros was invoked against Islam, the Catholic nun demonstrated with her Interior Castle a rapprochement with Islamic esoterism. In California, Santa Teresa is attached to a most unusual example of a Catholic sacred spring at the southern end of the San Francisco Bay. Legend holds that a

---

[99] Foothill Boulevard does, however, turn on its solitary course out of town to closely follow this azimuth after passing between Bishop Peak and Cerro San Luis.

[100] The location was reportedly named after its earliest Spanish landowner, Miguel Ávila.

[101] Cf. *Sacred Geography and the Paths of the Sun*, page 45.

mysterious woman in black had appeared in answer to the prayers of the Native people who were succumbing to disease, and that she had caused a spring to flow that would bring them healing. When the Spanish arrived, they interpreted the legend as referring to Santa Teresa, and to this day the waters of Santa Teresa Spring benefit visitors to Santa Teresa Park.[102] Whereas Saint James was named the Killer of Indians, Santa Teresa was remembered as a preserver of Native life.[103]

No doubt the padres had their own interpretation for having Mission San Luis Obispo in line with the solstices; but if this alignment was known to them, then doubtless the more dramatic alignment of the Nine Sisters was familiar to them as well. Within this landscape of power, both Native and Spanish perspectives shared an emphasis on the solstices, and both sought to be in alignment with cosmic forces. The affinity of these perspectives should not be downplayed, especially since it was recognized by the oldest Salinan report we have; and according to this report, there was good reason for this affinity:

> In 1773 a Salinan Indian woman (believed to be a centenarian) related to the San Antonio Mission padres that her grandfather told her stories about a man who visited their land upon four different occasions – each time arriving on the wings of a large bird. His clothes and

---

[102] Even with the relative ubiquity of the mystery walls, it is remarkable that examples of these cairns remain in the hills immediately to the south of the spring, with the nearest example aligned with the spring itself.

[103] The recent repainting of the mission church's interior includes shells as a nod to Spanish Catholicism, and this motif unfortunately reinforces the domination of Compostela over the memory of Santa Teresa.

teachings were identical to those of the mission San Antonio padres.[104]

Unfortunately, traditional efforts to align with cosmic forces have been eclipsed by other designs, but these designs only demonstrate further how the perspective of the Spanish padres was more in harmony with Native tradition than with the materialistic worldview of modern California.

---

[104] Betty War Brusa, *Salinan Indians of California and their Neighbors*, Happy Camp: Naturegraph, 2011, page 49. The winged transport of the visitor here recalls the griffins of legendary California.

6

Devil Canyon

California Polytechnic State University, or simply Cal Poly, is among the largest landowners in the Chorro Valley. Although this institution is dedicated to the application of science, obviously its aims are very different from the traditional science we have been considering. However, no one should imagine that modern science has no relationship with the traditional worlds. For example, if it is allowed that the dome of Morro Rock in its appearance suggests a Moorish dome, the modern development of Morro Bay may be seen to have given rise to its version of minarets. Instead of traditional signs of the Divine, however, that are erected like rays of light (*nūr*) as the name suggests, the three towers alongside the dome are the antitraditional signs of Morro Bay's failed power station (see following page).

Since the construction of the station in the mid-20th century, various owners have sought to profit by the generation of electrical power at the site, but the plant ceased all operations in 2014. At present, the plan is to bring down the smokestacks by 2028 and replace the old plant with the largest lithium-ion battery installation in the world. The towers may in themselves be a mockery, but it is also worth recognizing the irony of

Ottoman mosque of the 17th century (left)

seeking to generate electricity independent from and yet positioned upon the very alignment that dowsers would insist is already generating unsuspected electromagnetic power. As for the proposed battery installation, it likewise mocks the lava necks as bastions of that power.

A closer look at the ground plan of the power station reveals that it is rotated to face Morro Rock, in a manner recalling the "rotated" street grid of San Luis Obispo. In this position, however, the three smokestacks form an alignment with the next Sister in the chain, Black Hill. The power station alignment therefore supplants, in a sense, the alignment between Morro Rock and the other lava necks, but it is out of keeping with the solstitial azimuths. We have seen the harmful consequences that modern chemistry has had a upon the falcons of Morro Rock. It is at least worth reflecting on the impact that generating electrical power might have had on the natural order here, given its detrimental impact elsewhere; and without undue speculation, it is by no means clear what impact the artificial generation of energy might have upon the supernatural order. Surely it must be understood that for the Salinans, the "magnetism" of Morro Rock is inseparable from the rituals performed upon it.

Following the establishing of the mission, most of the modern development of the Nine Sisters landscape has been centered on San Luis Obispo. We now know that the azimuth of the winter solstice sunset leads from the city to the coast at the outer limits of Ávila Beach. By way of comparison, it is worth recalling the sacred geography of the Modoc people that I have explored in a series of essays,[105] and that from the Modoc heartlands the sacred height of Mount Shasta is plainly visible along that same sunset azimuth. Here, then, the ancient significance of the winter solstice as the "Door of Heaven" is evident. Disconcertingly near this solstitial alignment from San Luis Obispo, however, is another modern power station, in fact the last operational nuclear plant in California: Diablo Canyon. Its position is accentuated by its isolation along the coast, flagrantly oblivious to the danger presented by California's notorious fault lines since its planners were supposedly unaware of them. Attempts to have the facility decommissioned in recent years nearly proved successful, until the American president in late 2022 decided to grant Diablo Canyon over a

---

[105] See *Guardians of the Heart*.

billion dollars to continue supplying a significant percentage of California's electricity, at least for the time being.

Beyond the naming of the canyon after the Devil (*diablo*) instead of the "Door of Heaven,"[106] there is a deeper symbolism here that is mocked by nuclear power. In "The Modocs and a World's Heart," a petroglyph facing Mount Shasta upon the solstitial alignment was identified as a depiction of the Heart of the World that unites Heaven and earth (at left). Specifically, the split design at the head of the glyph signifies the bond between the sky lodge and earth lodge of the Old Man of the Ancients, with his earth lodge being Mount Shasta. The azimuth of the winter solstice sunset towards the sacred mountain is therefore directed towards the union of Heaven and earth. Their reintegration is nothing other than what John Michell described as "the fusion of earth energies with those of the cosmos." The atom is in Classical cosmology the most fundamental form of integrity; *atomos* in Greek literally means "indivisible." The nuclear process of fission, however, is dedicated to dividing the atom by force, and is the antithesis of fusion. There are further observations to be made here, including the use of Uranium and Plutonium as the particular agents of nuclear fission. Uranium is named for the Classical personification of the Sky, the equivalent of Caelus, whose name

---

[106] It is claimed that this designation inverts the region's traditional significance, and this is likely, given other examples such as the sacred mountain in California called Mount Diablo. Concerning its ancient importance, the archaeological report of what was swept away by development was published as *9000 Years of Prehistory at Diablo Canyon*.

would therefore be known to the ancient Pythagoreans. Plutonium is named after the Roman god of the Underworld, and we have already referred to the summer solstice as the Door of the Underworld. Indeed, Uranium and Plutonium are names that correspond perfectly to the respective Latin names of the solstitial doors; yet their use does not benefit souls, but results only in material power and poisons much more terrible than that of serpents. The two domes of Devil Canyon (above) rise like pseudo-Morros designed to counter the "stimulation of spirit."

The development of nuclear energy was inseparable from its military application, and California played a pivotal role in this history. Plutonium was discovered and named by scientists from the University of California at Berkeley,[107] and

---

[107] I have noted the unusual geology of the site chosen for the Berkeley Laboratory in the context of the mystery walls (*Guardians of the Heart*,

the "Father of the Atomic Bomb," J. Robert Oppenheimer, was likewise a scientist at Berkeley before he was chosen to head the Los Alamos Laboratory in New Mexico as its first director. The activities at Los Alamos were codenamed Project Y, and given the Pythagorean significance of the Paths of the Sun, it is worth observing that Y was long considered the "Pythagoric letter."[108] The traditional interpretation of the letter's form focused on the choice between two paths, that of virtue and that of vice, with Hercules serving as the heroic exemplar who chose only the path of virtue. There may originally have been a choice at Los Alamos, but under Oppenheimer, the path taken was not that of Hercules but rather that of Prometheus.

On the occasion of the first nuclear explosion, Oppenheimer was famously reported to have quoted from Hindu scripture. "Now I am become Death, the destroyer of worlds" are the words ascribed to him, and is Oppenheimer's translation from the *Bhagavad Gita* of the declaration by Krishna, the avatar of Vishnu. Krishna spoke these words while revealing his divine form, and did so in order to convince the archer Arjuna of the need to make war to preserve order in the world. It would seem that Oppenheimer was invoking these words as justification for his work. However, and without disputing that he did many years later admit that these words did come to his mind, the quote is only what is popularly recalled; in fact, these words were secondary to another passage he quoted from the same sacred source: "If the radiance of a thousand suns were to burst at once into the sky, that would be like the splendor of the

---

page 52). It should also be recalled that these structures were formerly known as the "Berkeley Mystery Walls" due to their concentration there, although only one example has apparently survived to the present day.

[108] Cf. *Paths of the Western Sun* volume I, op. cit., page 74.

mighty one."[109] Leaving aside the traditional context of Krishna's advice – a tradition to which the scientist did not in any real sense belong – the reported "disconcerting triumphalism" with which Oppenheimer conducted himself in the aftermath of the test is revealing testimony.[110] For now it is enough to admit that Oppenheimer used solar imagery explicitly to celebrate his Promethean accomplishment.[111]

Clearly, the expression "a thousand suns" conveys a qualitative rather than a quantitative value, and serves to indicate the superiority of spiritual over physical splendor; yet the expression presupposes the correspondence between light and spiritual presence in traditional symbolism. In the Old Testament of Oppenheimer's ancestors, the prophet Moses descended from Mount Sinai with the Divine Revelation to his people and his face shone so brightly that it had to be veiled.[112] Obviously this may be compared to the unveiling of Vishnu in the *Bhagavad Gita*; Arabic translations of the Tantric *Pool of Amrita* even insist on the spiritual equivalence between Moses and Vishnu. Moses appears luminous again in the New Testament, alongside Elijah and Jesus during the Transfiguration upon Mount Tabor.[113] Oppenheimer personally codenamed the first nuclear test "Trinity," which obviously recalls Christianity before all else. Orientalism also posited a "trinity" for Hinduism, comprised of Brahma, Vishnu, and

---

[109] These words provided the title of Robert Jungk's book from 1958, *Brighter Than a Thousand Suns: A Personal History of the Atomic Scientists* (New York: Harcourt Brace).

[110] See Ray Monk, *Robert Oppenheimer: A Life Inside the Center*, New York: Doubleday, 2012, pages 457 and 467.

[111] The subsequent development of thermonuclear weapons involved combining the process of fusion to that of fission, and nuclear fusion is the very process that physicists attribute to the Sun.

[112] Book of Exodus 34:29.

[113] All three of the so-called "Synoptic Gospels" include reports of the event, although Mount Tabor is not specifically named.

Shiva, and Vishnu's inclusion may therefore be compared with the involvement of Moses in the Transfiguration. However, Oppenheimer claimed that the source of the codename was somehow derived from the Holy Sonnets of the poet John Donne, though what the scientist specifically meant by this is obscure. Donne was, of course, an Anglican cleric of the 17th century, and it is not surprising that he would have referenced the Transfiguration, the appearance of a "trinity" of persons to the Apostles in luminous splendor. Oppenheimer's focus on rivalling Vishnu's divine disclosure may help identify, then, his choice of "Trinity" as an oblique reference to the Transfiguration, the comparable event in the Gospels.[114] Of course, his evocation of Vishnu eclipses any obvious reference to the light of Moses, but it is indeed curious that Oppenheimer would substitute Vishnu for the spirituality of a prophet that Islamic esoterism associates with him. Regardless, if it is clear enough that the name of Uranium mocks everything heavenly, Oppenheimer's words should be understood to define the development of nuclear weapons by the Christian world as a counterfeit Transfiguration.

○

In the landscape of the Nine Sisters, there was a science involved in the placement and positioning of the mission; the subsequent locating of the anti-Christic power station in Avila Beach seems to have been no less precise. Just as an evil practitioner of Tantrism could be called a "a sorcerer," the name "Diablo Canyon" openly declares the sorcery at work in

---

[114] The illusion of human technology surpassing spiritual realization has reached its fullest development in "transhumanism."

exploiting a sacred landscape.[115] If the experience of a harmonious landscape may lead to spiritual awareness, disruptions in the physical domain must also have an effect on the psyche, and often enough prevent the soul from being illuminated by the realm of the spirit. These disruptions, then, constitute a kind of sorcery since they are opposed to saintly illumination, and modern science is very much to blame for disrupting the harmony in our landscape environments. The doctrine of the Paths of the Sun reveals the value of certain landscapes to the fate of souls, and disruptions along these paths must be especially harmful.

Prior to the construction of the power plant at Diablo Canyon, there were developments in the wider region that suggest the value of its specific location. Extending a solstice azimuth along the coast from Diablo Canyon demonstrates that the coastline itself, like the nearby line of the Nine Sisters, approximates this astronomical alignment to a remarkable degree. After the coastline shifts again to the south, the region in line with this azimuth is near the town of Oceano, and this place is noteworthy for a number of reasons. Extending from Oceano to the south is a vast expanse of sand dunes with the tallest examples on the West Coast. Cecil B. DeMille used this landscape for his original film of *The Ten Commandments*, and set pieces from the production actually ended up being buried in these sands.[116] More importantly, the dunes served as the setting for a self-sufficient community of non-conformists in the mid-20th century. The so-called Dunites included artists, writers, and the son of a former president, as well as an early proponent of

---

[115] The Trinity nuclear test was conducted at White Sands, and it should not be surprising to find that this place was important to Native tradition.
[116] Here again is an echo of the presence of Moses.

Veganism. In nearby Halcyon,[117] a Theosophical school and community had been established at the end of the 19th century. Both the Bohemian Dunites and the Theosophists were convinced of the region's unique energies.

A unique record of the Dunites may be found in the semi-autobiographical novel *Fairy Tales are True* by the adventurer and engineer Shamcher Bryn Beorse. Beorse was born in Norway and traveled widely, becoming a practitioner of yoga. The name Shamcher, however, declares his attachment to the Sufi tradition, in particular the lineage transmitted by the earliest emissary of Sufism in America, Hazrat Inayat Khan of India. In his novel, Beorse describes the dunes as a "paradise" and "a place where time stood still."[118] He applies the terms of spirituality in India to individual Dunites and connects them with the festival known as Kumbha Mela. Leaving aside its modern development, it is worth recognizing that this festival commemorates the mythology of the "Churning of the Sea of Milk" that was described above in connection with the nine planets. What is more, the meeting of yoga and Sufism was precisely the milieu to which I linked the doctrine of the nine yoginis.

These coincidences do more than testify to the relevance of these themes to California. It would seem that Beorse, through his initiatory preparedness, was able to interpret a landscape that was not merely physical. This unseen landscape need not be identified as spiritual. After all, neither the Theosophists nor the Dunites should be mistaken for

---

[117] Ovid relates the expression "Halcyon Days" to a period of calm at the time of the winter solstice, which is clearly a memory of the *janua coeli*. It is worth noting that the Theosophical school at Halcyon, like that of Lomaland in San Diego, was founded and led by a woman.

[118] Shamcher Bryn Beorse, *Fairy Tales are True: Silent Reach from the Dunes to the Kumbha Mela*, Vancouver: Alpha Glyph Publications, 2014, page 39.

representatives of traditional integrity; yet the dunes seem to have been a place where psychic energies were focused. Before long, however, oil was discovered and extracted from the dunes, and much of the sands have since been turned over to the ravages of recreational vehicles. Even so, it is worth acknowledging that the mysteries of the dunes only surfaced prior to the disruptions of Diablo Canyon, and that the modern power plant remains upon a landscape that relates both to bodies and to souls.

The landscape of Mission Carmel
prior to modern developments

7

Custodians of Holy Lands

In both the Old Testament account of Moses and the New Testament accounts of the Transfiguration, spiritual light manifests upon a mountain.[119] Curiously, the same name in Arabic – *Jabal Tūr* - is applied both to Mount Sinai that dominates the sacred history of Moses and Mount Tabor, the traditional site of the Transfiguration. With the epigraph to his study on the Franciscan "liturgy of light" in a California mission of the 19th century, Rubén Mendoza indicates that the solar illuminations belong to the theme of the Transfiguration: "And he was transfigured before them, and his face shone like the sun, and his garments became white as light."[120] It is therefore of

---

[119] This theme is most apparent in the "Mountain of Light" (*Jabal Nūr*) of the Islamic tradition, where the "last testament" of the Holy Qur'an was revealed; however, in keeping with Islam's final position in this temporal cycle, the complementary symbolism of the cave is preeminent (cf. René Guénon, "The Mountain and the Cave," *Symbols of Sacred Science*, op. cit.).

[120] "The Liturgy of Light: Solar Geometry and Kinematic Liturgical Iconography in an Early 19th Century California Mission," *Boletín: The Journal of the California Mission Studies Association*, volume 28, numbers 1 and 2, 2011 and 2012, page 8.

particular interest that in the early 20th century, the Franciscan Order constructed a Church of the Transfiguration upon Mount Tabor in the Holy Land that included a most remarkable feature. Every year to mark the Feast of the Transfiguration on 6 August, sunlight is reflected from a mirror in the floor of the church to shine upon a mosaic above the altar that depicts the Transfiguration.

There are other signs that the site conforms to a sacred plan. The axis of the present church is oriented north of west, seemingly to be in harmony with the axis of the hill; but it must at the same time be observed that this orientation approximates the azimuth of sunset on 6 August. Most remarkable of all, perhaps, is the fact that this azimuth leads directly to Carmel and the Mountain of Lord Elijah (*Jabal Mar Ilyas*).[121] Elijah's participation in the Transfiguration is therefore indicated through sacred geography, and the Christian fixing of the festival upon 6 August betrays a subtle wisdom that did not have its origin with the Franciscans, though they did their part to preserve it. [122]

---

[121] The prophet Elijah is not an Abrahamic form of Helios, although in Greek their names are quite similar, and the fiery vehicle of his ascension does recall the solar chariot of Helios. According to the tradition of Islam, Elijah ascended on a horse of fire instead of a chariot; yet Islamic esoterism insists on associating him closely with Idris or Enoch, whose solar identity is clear (cf. *Alchemy in Middle-earth*, op. cit., pages ix and 20-1). More exactly, Islamic esoterism regards Jesus and Elijah, along with Idris and the Green Man who instructs Moses (*Qur'an* XVIII, 60-82), as the chiefs of the spiritual hierarchy called the Awtad; on the Awtad and the symbolism of mountains, see *The Red and the White*, chapter 5.

[122] The earliest marking of the festival is attributed to the Nestorians (Ignatius Puthiadam, *Christian Liturgy*, Mumbai: Saint Pauls, 2003, page 169); on the Nestorians, see René Guénon, *The King of the World*, op. cit., page 9.

Given the rather recent construction of the church, it is tempting to imagine that the Franciscan Order decided to apply on Mount Tabor what it had already carried out in California with its solar illuminations, despite the geographic separation. However, it is worth remembering that a comparable illumination from an earlier period has been observed in Chartres cathedral that moreover involves the floor, a characteristic not specifically found in California. At Chartres, a "signature" of sorts is found in the source of the light that shines upon the floor, since it passes through a window dedicated to Saint Apollinaris. Aside from its context in the history of the Church, this name signifies "Holy Apollo," and there is every reason to recognize here a reference to the Pythagoreans.[123]

The involvement of the Franciscans in aligning with solar illuminations therefore seems to follow the example of the Pythagoreans in the Holy Land, who were likewise an initiatory order. The sacred principle to which the Pythagoreans were attached was named Apollo, and his presence is symbolically at the center of the Nine Muses as well as along the Path of the Sun through Europe. Remarkably, by tracing this Pythagorean Axis of Saint Michael and of Apollo from Carmel, it is possible to discover the foundations of the Franciscan Order. Saint Francis was considered nothing less than a "Second Christ" in Medieval Europe, and though he travelled widely in keeping with the example of Jesus, he was born and died in the Italian town of Assisi that is precisely upon this Path of the Sun. What is more, his travels included a visit to the cavern sanctuary of Gargano at the "midpoint" of the Axis, and the saint's conduct at the cavern betrays an intimate knowledge of the reality of that place, and so, perhaps, of the Path through it.[124] Since the wolf was considered an animal sacred to Apollo, the pact between Saint Francis and the Wolf of Gubbio that features in his hagiography

---

[123] See "The Labyrinth of the Age of Gold" in *Guardians of the Heart*.
[124] See *Sacred Geography and the Paths of the Sun*, pages 36 and 111.

St. Francis and the Sultan[125]
Robert Lentz, OFM

---

[125] The script in the Franciscan icon is the second verse of the Holy Qur'an: "Praise be to Allāh, Lord of the Worlds."

assumes greater significance, especially since Gubbio is also positioned along the Axis of Saint Michael and of Apollo.

In addition to the story of the wolf, Saint Francis' patronage of the natural world is demonstrated by his sermon to the birds. Even though the interpretation of the event in the Medieval *Little Flowers of Saint Francis* seems to offer more to his human followers than to the birds, it is worth recalling the legendary "Language of the Birds" in this context. In Norse legend, the hero Sigurd learns this language following his defeat of the dragon Fafnir; and in the defeat of the two-headed serpent at Morro Rock, Falcon and Raven must have spoken this language to each other. The Holy Qur'an makes explicit reference to this mysterious language, but it is another passage that is worth relating to the conduct of Saint Francis; and it should be very clear that this Islamic teaching is eminently at home in the Native milieu:

> *There is not an animal in the earth, nor a flying creature flying on two wings, but they are peoples like unto you. We have neglected nothing in the Book (of Our decrees). Then unto their Lord they will be gathered.*[126]

In recent years, the mysterious meeting between Saint Francis and the Muslim ruler al-Malik al-Kamil in Egypt has been held up as a model of religious reconciliation, for example in the icon "St. Francis and the Sultan" by the Franciscan Robert Lentz. This scene, however, only illustrates a teaching found in the Qur'an itself concerning religious communities:

> *...And thou wilt find the nearest of them in affection to those who believe (to be) those who say: Lo! We are*

---

[126] VI, 38.

Christians. That is because there are among them priests and monks, and because they are not proud.[127]

Perhaps a consequence of this reconciliation with Islam was that the Franciscan order would ever after be accorded the role of Custodians of the Holy Land for the Roman Catholic church.[128]

At the present time, the leadership of the Catholic church belongs to the first pope from the Americas and the first to be called Francis. Pope Francis' liberal leanings have caused some controversy, but his championing of the poor and the natural world not only follows the example of Saint Francis, but is especially important in a time marked by economic disparity and ecological imbalance. Among the more controversial decisions of Pope Francis was plainly out of keeping with liberal politics, however, and pertained to Native America in particular: his canonization of Father Junipero Serra.[129] Serra is now officially recognized as the Apostle of California, having served as President-General of the Missions of Alta California between 1769 and 1784 and personally having founded nine of them.[130] Pope Francis announced the confirmation of Father Serra's sainthood in 2015 during his first visit to North America. Among other things, this confirmation transformed the Carmel mission where he was buried into the shrine of a Roman Catholic saint.

Mission Carmel was only the second mission to be

---

[127] V, 82.

[128] Louis Massignon, who was a tertiary of the Franciscan order, made his vow of the *Badaliya* at the church in Damietta where Saint Francis had met with the sultan, a vow which aimed to further the reconciliation of Christians with Islam.

[129] The name "Serra," like the word "sierra," may be used to refer to a serrated line of mountain peaks, and so also to the Nine Sisters.

[130] Serra began by founding a mission in Baja. The total number of missions in Alta California, excluding the missions of San Rafael and Sonoma for reasons already given, is 19.

established in Alta California under Serra's guidance, the year after Mission San Diego. Carmel served as headquarters for the missions of Alta California because that was Serra's favorite place and where he chose to reside. Above the entrance to the church, a window in the form of a rayed
orb was positioned to face the rising Sun on the summer solstice. This window now illuminates the shrine of a saint (above), but it is more than likely that the solar testimony of Mission Carmel was always known to the Apostle of California. For that matter, as President-General, Serra of all people would have been in the position to direct the missionaries' mysterious architectural agenda.

In this context, then, there is more to the naming of Mission Carmel than is commonly supposed. The mission is actually dedicated to San Carlos Borromeo of Milan, who is not associated with Carmel in the Holy Land. Its continued designation as Mission Carmel derives rather from the nearby river that for some reason was named for the holy mountain before the arrival of the Franciscans. Since the first Spaniard to arrive in the region was Vizcaino, it is assumed that the name "Carmel" was inspired by the three Carmelite friars who accompanied his voyage. The Carmelite Order was in turn named for the holy mountain, and because of the pious example of Pythagoras in that place the Carmelites actually considered him as well as Elijah as their founders.[131] For this reason, it is

---

[131] See *Sacred Geography and the Paths of the Sun*, page 45. The choice of the name "Carmel" further recalls the most influential representative of the Carmelites, Santa Teresa, whose Castle of the Soul resonates so intimately with the mythology of California.

remarkable indeed that the orientation of Mission Carmel marks the Sun's position at the solstices. At the eastern edge of Europe, the alignment from Mount Carmel is towards the summer solstice sunset. At the western edge of the Americas, the mission church both receives the light of midsummer sunrise while its head actually faces the setting Sun at the winter solstice. Of course, this last point brings Mission Carmel as the shrine of a saint into perfect accord with Pythagorean doctrine, since the winter solstice was considered the *janua coeli* reserved for the elect. Pope Francis' recognition of Saint Junipero Serra therefore serves to confirm this Pythagorean legacy in California.

If the church on Mount Tabor helps shed light on the Franciscans' role as Custodians of the Holy Land, the illuminations in the missions testify that the order served in a comparable role in California, where its sacred landscape provided a path not to sorcery, but to sainthood.

O

As for Pope Francis, his real importance only comes into focus if we acknowledge his position in the so-called "Prophecy of the Popes." Through a series of 112 mysterious mottos, this document attributed to Saint Malachy of Ireland explains the identities of the popes remaining from his time in the Middle Ages until the ending of the world. The document is officially downplayed by the Catholic Church, perhaps because a simple tally results in Pope Francis being identified as the last in the list of 112, and the pope who will preside over the fall of Rome.[132]

---

[132] However, as recently as 1958 an American candidate for the papacy sailed upon the river Tiber on a boat filled with sheep to demonstrate his eligibility to be *"pastor et nautor"* in accordance with the motto for the next pope.

Supporters of this 'prophecy" have long been at pains to associate each motto with the corresponding pope, and the motto attached to Pope Francis is no doubt obscure, since he is called "Peter the Roman." Charles-André Gilis, Guénon continuator, has offered that the mottos of the prophecy should really be calculated as 111 + 1, since the motto of Peter the Roman concerns the end of a world and therefore the beginning of the next.[133] This is, of course, suggested by the name of the last pope, since the name "Peter the Roman" also belongs to the first pope. Here, then, is the key to understanding how this name could pertain to Francis. Just as Saint Francis was considered a "Second Christ," Pope Francis corresponds to a "Second Peter." In any case, it is certainly worth recognizing that despite attempts to ignore this contribution of Saint Malachy, or to explain away its unequivocal calculation, the Prophecy of the Popes testifies to the imminent ending of the world.

---

[133] Charles-André Gilis, *Qâf et les Mystères du Coran Glorieux*, Beirut: Albouraq, 2006, page 207. Gilis focuses on the importance of Pope Benedict XVI, Francis' predecessor, since the number 111 is attached to him. This number is associated with the supreme spiritual authority in Islamic esoterism; in *Sacred Geography and the Paths of the Sun* I considered the example of Shaykh Nazim al-Haqqani as an embodiment of that authority. Remarkably, Benedict met with al-Haqqani on the island of Cyprus shortly before the pope's rather unique abdication.

A modern statue of Saint Junipero Serra near San Francisco
Despite Serra's travels north and south, this strange monument points
to the west. It is now closed to the public, no doubt out of fear that it
will continue to be targeted by other than transcendent principles.

8

Occidentation

The conquest of the Americas by the Spanish – and make no mistake, the Spanish came as *conquistadores* or "conquerors" – brought a cataclysm of seemingly apocalyptic proportions. In the context of the traditional doctrine of temporal cycles, an apocalypse refers to the "disclosure" that comes at the closing of a given cycle, and this disclosure necessarily includes an intrusion of superior influences. According to the Hindu doctrines, there are four ages or *Yugas*, with each being worse than the preceding, and this corresponds exactly to the Classical succession of Golden Age, Silver Age, Bronze Age, and Iron Age. According to both systems, a cyclic return to the first age follows the death of the fourth, though this return is never a simple matter of repetition, and the superior influences present at the end of a cycle really belong to the beginning of the next. The Classical expectation that a new Golden Age would follow the end of the Iron Age was formulated in Virgil's Fourth Ecologue, which further defined this expectation even into the Middle Ages, as I have described elsewhere.[134] With this in mind, it should be recognized that the

---

[134] See especially "The Labyrinth of the Age of Gold" in *Guardians of the Heart*.

The Nine Sisters of California

Native cataclysm was not strictly apocalyptic, since forces with weapons of iron overwhelmed a "stone age" civilization, whereas an apocalypse would have involved the death of the Iron Age. No doubt Native death was catastrophic, and signaled the end of the world they had known; yet this death only brought them into a worsening age, which is profoundly tragic. For the Spanish, the "primordiality" of Native civilization may be the real reason why they were obsessed by finding cities of gold; in reality they sought the Golden Age that they knew was just over the horizon.

In terms of number, René Guénon has explained the duration of the four *Yugas* or ages of time of Hindu doctrine in relation to a principal symbol of the Pythagoreans. This symbol is the Tetraktys (below), a representation of the "triangular number" of four. Guénon observes that $1 + 2 + 3 + 4 = 10$, and continues: "If the numbers are taken in the reverse order: $4 + 3 + 2 + 1$, this gives the proportions of the four *Yugas*, the sum of which is the denary, that is to say the final and complete cycle."[135] Here we return to the significance of the denary, that we related above

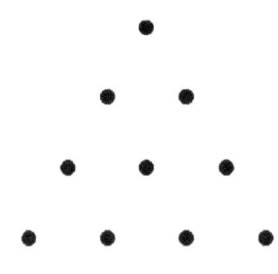

to the circular symbol of the Sun. This relationship is further indicated by the motif of ten Suns that "emerge from unity at the beginning of the cycle and re-enter it at the end."[136] Once again it is worth recalling the Chinese legend of Fusang that involves Yi the Archer shooting down nine Suns, as well as its analogue

---

[135] *The Reign of Quantity and the Signs of the Times*, Translated by Lord Northbourne, Baltimore: Penguin, 1972, page 346.
[136] René Guénon, *The Symbolism of the Cross*, Hillsdale: Sophia Perennis, 2001, page 61.

among the Shasta people of the Oregon borderlands.[137] As I commented in *The Red and the White*, the shooting of the nine to leave one is an expression of a return to the center; only now we may add that this return involves the beginning of a temporal cycle.

Since the beginnings of Roman Christianity, the Fourth Ecologue of Virgil was interpreted as foretelling the birth of Jesus Christ; and within the prophecy of the Sibyl of Apollo, there are indeed signs of the Pythagorean understanding of the "Door of Heaven:" "Now from high heaven a new generation comes down." Of course, the Franciscans in California knew the winter solstice in terms of the festival of Christ's birth, and the ancient understanding of the *janua coeli* as the way of the gods had been subsumed by the teaching that "no man cometh unto the Father, but by me."[138] However, it now appears that the architectural emphasis on the solstices at the missions was part of a special veneration of the solar Christ, and that this veneration directed evangelization efforts that "constitute a sanctified conflation, cultural accommodation, and spiritual reconciliation of both pre-Columbian and European cosmologies."[139] To be fair, the Spanish were not the first to orient their churches to the solstices. There are Medieval examples in northern Wales that demonstrate this,[140] but these "solstitial churches" always preserve an eastern orientation.

---

[137] See *The Red and the White*, pages 72-3. The Salinan legend of Morro Rock that involves the cutting up of the serpent by the archer and monster hunter Prairie-Falcon may be a variant of the same theme.

[138] Book of John 14:6.

[139] Mendoza 2011 and 2012, page 16.

[140] See Bernadette Brady, "The Dual Alignments of the Solstitial Churches in North Wales," *Journal of Skyscape Archaeology*, volume 3 number 1, 2017. In the case of Wales we have suspected the direct influence of Pythagoreanism; cf. "Idris in Wales" in *Guardians of the Heart*, page 71.

By complete contrast, the most persistent characteristic of the mission churches is their reversing of the directional norm, or their "occidentation" instead of "orientation." For his part, Rubén Mendoza does not dwell on the implications of the mission churches' reversal. As a Catholic, he may very well prefer not to draw attention to such an about-face. This reversal hardly seems necessitated in all cases by the solar illuminations. Rarely does the meridian or nave of a church align with the solstice sunrise as at the Carmel mission; and if it is simply a window that is the source of the specific illumination, there is no need for the door of the church to be at one end rather than the other. The nave of a church is so-called because of the symbolism of navigation, and so it is unclear why a course would so often be set for the west, unless the Native belief in the western Land of the Dead was being accommodated.

Although "occidentation" is not a focus of his scholarship, Mendoza admits the existence of "now largely unexplained and largely unexplored 'hidden traditions'"[141] within the California missions. Among these "hidden traditions," the Pythagorean doctrine of the solstices as gateways allows us to recognize how the solstitial emphasis of the solar illuminations relates to the Franciscan commitment to "serve as the gatekeepers of the impending apocalypse." Indeed, the reversal of mission churches in California must also be viewed as an expression of the millenarian beliefs of the Franciscan Order, especially because of its rapprochement with Islam; for there is no clearer formulation of apocalyptic occidentation than the Tradition in Islam that the Sun will ultimately rise in the west.

According to Islamic orthodoxy, the "sun rising from the place of its setting" is among the five principal signs of the End of Time. This event is synonymous with the so-called "reversal of the poles" to which René Guénon sometimes

---

[141] Mendoza 2005, page 109.

referred, and Guénon's continuator characterizes this reversal as belonging to the symbolism of the serpent.[142] For Islamic esoterism, the image of the western sunrise indicates the most noble descendant of the Prophet Muhammad who is called al-Mahdi and who gathers the faithful in preparation for the return of Jesus. This is the significance of the title of the book by the *Shaykh al-akbar* or "Greatest Master" of Islamic esoterism, Ibn `Arabi: *`Anqa' mughrib fi ma`rifat khatm al-awliya' wa shams al-maghrib* ("The Wondrous Anqa in the Knowledge of the Seal of Saints and the Sun of the West").[143] According to Islamic Tradition, al-Mahdi is expected to "fill the earth with justice as it had been filled with injustice," and this too constitutes a reversal.

Al-Mahdi is called the "Caliph of God," a title that is explicitly given to Adam the first man in the Holy Qur'an;[144] and so the appearance of al-Mahdi at the end of this cycle signals a return to the primordial state embodied at its beginning. According to Islamic esoterism, there is a language associated with Adam and so with the primordial state, the *lughat suryāniyyah* or "Syriac Language." Rumors of this language's power have long haunted occultists, including the Elizabethan

---

[142] Gilis 2005, pages 20-1.

[143] The "Seal of Saints" may refer either to the "Seal of Universal Sainthood," who is Jesus, or to the "Seal of Muhammadan Sainthood" who is believed to have been Ibn `Arabi himself. The Anqa is a giant bird of Arab legendry, easily compared to the giant bird in the Salinan account of the mysterious visitor; and Gerald Elmore argues his case for translating anqa as "gryphon" in *Islamic Sainthood in the Fullness of Time* (Leiden: Brill, 1999, pages 184-6). This book also contains a description of a microcosmic city as a circle with concentric walls (ibid., pages 579, 586-7), and since the Shaykh was born in Medieval Spain, his description provides an immediate prefiguration of the circular castle of Santa Teresa.

[144] II, 30; on the mysteries of the caliphate, see Charles-André Gilis, *Les Sept Étendards de Califat*, Paris: Éditions Traditionnelles, 1993.

magus Dr. John Dee. Very remarkably in the present context, René Guénon defines this language as being that of "solar illuminations (*shams ishrāqiyyah*)," and points out that Surya is the Sanskrit name of the Sun;[145] he also associates this language with the legendary "Language of the Birds." This Syriac Language seems to have its eschatological counterpart in the mysterious *Jafr* that al-Mahdi is expected to interpret and that expresses "an esoteric science based on the symbolism of letters and numbers,"[146] a description that justifiably recalls Pythagoreanism. All are rooted in the Science of Letters, and the power of this science in the world depends upon the identity of the latter as a vast book. As far as it concerns our subject, it may be offered that Arabic letters are composed of lines as well as points, and so geomantic elements such as landscape alignments, mystery walls or linear cairns and sacred points or seats may offer correspondences related to this same arcane science.[147]

Shaykh Muhyiddin Ibn ʿArabi, who was an exact contemporary of Saint Francis, examines the highest meanings of the Science of Letters in his writings, and provides a wealth of knowledge about al-Mahdi and the ending of this world. After relating the expectation that al-Mahdi will rule for five, seven, or nine years, the Shaykh focuses on the last number by enumerating the nine characteristics of the spiritual station of

---

[145] "The Science of Letters (*Ilm al-hurūf*)," *Symbols of Sacred Science*, op. cit. It may be admitted that the word for "illuminations" here relates to the east rather than the west, in keeping with its primordial character.

[146] This phrase is translated from Michel Vâlsan's definition in Abd Ar-Razzâq Al-Qâshânî, *Les Lettres-Isolées du Coran*, Bamako: Éditions Sagesse et Tradition, 2007, page 34.

[147] See ibid. on the world as a vast book. To shed light on the structures of geomancy, it may be noted that the Arabic word for a chapter of the Holy Qur'an, *surah*, also signifies a "wall."

his "Helpers."¹⁴⁸ These characteristics are essentially the qualifications for exercising power in the spiritual governance of the world (*tasarruf*). Since these nine characteristics belong to the Mahdi above all, they may be imagined in accordance with the circular significance of nine around the central position of the Caliph of God. However, there is a testimony expressed in the Traditions that "There is no Mahdi if not Jesus," owing to their inseparability, and this relationship is expressed by the two half-circumferences that necessarily belong to the circular symbol of the Sun.¹⁴⁹ If the implementation of sacred power in the world is a right of the Mahdi, it belongs in its fullness to Jesus who alone has the power to slay the Antichrist. This role of Jesus is identified in Christianity as the *sol justitiae*, the "Sun of Justice," while in Hinduism the Solar Christ is "the tenth or Kalki avatar, who is to come at the end of the cycle, the 'white horse' of this final descent being a solar symbol par excellence."¹⁵⁰ Here again with the tenth avatar of Vishnu we

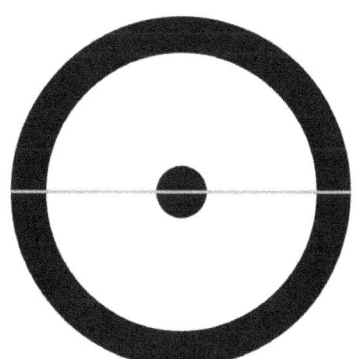

The two half-circumferences
of the solar circle

---

¹⁴⁸ See "At the End of Time" translated by James W. Morris in Ibn al `Arabi, *The Meccan Openings*, New York: Pir Press, 2002, pages 72 ff.
¹⁴⁹ Gilis 1993, pages 289-90.
¹⁵⁰ René Guénon, *Traditional Forms and Cosmic Cycles*, Hillsdale: Sophia Perennis, 2003, page 84.

find the denary expressing a return to the center and the luminous power of the Sun.

In *Alchemy in Middle-earth*, I mentioned details about al-Mahdi that have been provided by contemporary masters of Islamic esoterism, and two details are worth repeating here. First, he is described as being surrounded by 99 Caliphs, here meaning "representatives," which despite the double digits indicates again the circular significance of nine. Second, he is described as being in occultation inside a cave, and so within the earth.[151] With this information we may contrast the earthly position of al-Mahdi with the heavenly position of Jesus before his descent. Just as the fusion of earth energies with those of the cosmos was the concern of ancient science, the restoration of the primordial state in the world requires the participation of al-Mahdi from the earth and Jesus from the sky, and the fusion of these domains is symbolized by the two half-circumferences of the solar circle.

Having returned to the circularity of nine, it should not be ignored that there happens to be an eschatological aspect to the archetype of the Castle of Maidens, even if that aspect remains obscure. Henry Corbin notes the presence of this archetype in the eschatology of Ancient Persia, where it is attached to a figure named Bahram Varjavand: "Certain traditions specify that he will come from the 'city of the maidens' (*shahr-i dukhtarān*) which lies in the direction of Tibet." In keeping with his thesis, Corbin muses on the "homologation of the Zoroastrian eschatological hero to the person of the hidden Imām," by which he means the Mahdi; but because of Persian geography, he speculates that the City of Maidens could be "an allusion to the kingdom of Amazons to the north of India

---

[151] Op. cit., pages 95-6. It should not be overlooked that the occultation of the Mahdi corresponds exactly with the legendary sleep of King Arthur within the earth, and that the latter is simply another formulation of his healing in Avalon.

referred to in Chinese chronicles."[152] In this context, it would be better to point out the similarities between the Nine Sisters of Avalon and this city of maidens, especially since it is from Avalon that King Arthur, healed of his wounds, must return.

Regardless, what is essential here is that the "eschatological hero" must emerge from the spiritual center, while the direction of the center must vary depending upon the viewpoint of a given traditional world in its time and place. Just as the Celtic Otherworld was associated with the west, as we have already noted, a similar occidentation may be said to belong both to Islamic eschatology as well as to the perspective of the California missions. This recalls the remarkable compatibility between the traditional perspectives of the Ancient Celts, Christianity, and Islam that happened to give rise to the Medieval flowering of Arthurian literature, a subject to which I intend to return.[153]

O

The era between the lifetime of Father Serra and his official canonization brought genocide and the complete collapse of Native society in California, but this may not be blamed wholly on the padres whose presence in California was

---

[152] Henry Corbin, *Spiritual Body and Celestial Earth: From Mazdean Iran to Shī'ite Iran*, Princeton: Princeton University Press, 1977, pages 70, 292 note 126.

[153] This "compatibility" is likewise expressed In *The Lord of the Rings*, in which the only explicit demonstration of religious ritual involves turning to face the west (cf. *Alchemy in Middle-earth*, pages 98-9). It might also be insisted that the ultimate realization of the Ringbearer is described in terms seemingly alluding to a solar reversal: he is sailing west into "a swift sunrise" when it is by moving towards the sun that its rising is made swift.

so short lived. Indeed, secular materialism has proven to be the enemy of all traditional peoples, Native and Abrahamic alike. This materialism has unified the world according to its doctrines and has left little room for traditional knowledge. Its legacy has been to sunder earth energies from those of the cosmos and so prevent the stimulation of spirit. Is it any wonder, then, that the return of the spirit should come as a complete reversal? Still, materialism must serve its purpose, as René Guénon explains:

> ...the "solidification" of the world appears to some extent to have a double meaning: considered in itself and from within the cycle...it evidently has an "unfavourable" significance, "sinister" and opposed to spirituality; but, in another aspect, it is nonetheless necessary in order to prepare, though it be in a manner which could be called "negative," the ultimate fixation of the results of the cycle in the form of the "Heavenly Jerusalem," where these results will at once become the germs of the possibilities of the future cycle. Nevertheless, it goes without saying that in the final fixation itself, and in order that it may indeed become a restoration of the "primordial state," the immediate intervention of a transcendent principle in necessary, otherwise nothing could be saved and the "cosmos" would simply evaporate into "chaos." It is this intervention which produces the final "reversal"...[154]

Prior to this intervention, materialism has facilitated the replacement of traditional understanding with something else

---

[154] Guénon 1972, page 175.

entirely. In a remarkable passage about a resident of the Oceano dunes, Shamcher Bryn Beorse refers to the belief in Lemuria, an imaginary "lost continent" of the Pacific that according to the Theosophists was older than Atlantis:

> He could not even keep to the present, but made frequent forays into past dune lore and the legends of some early squatter who had lived in the dunes while waiting for ancient Lemuria to rise up out of the Pacific Ocean. These long-ago residents seem to have spent most of their time on the beach, breathing in chorus and sighing, "Lemuria" into the west. To their astonished disappointment, Lemuria did not appear, but they remained sure that it eventually would.[155]

As I have noted elsewhere, the name "Lemuria" is ultimately derived from Lemures, the ghosts of the dead in ancient Rome, and in this respect the belief in Lemuria mimics the Native understanding of a western land of the dead.[156] The Ghost Dance of Native tradition sought to bring about the final "reversal," and so the hopes of the Dunites may be compared with it, even if there could be no question here of authentic ritual. The supposed antiquity of Lemuria suggests that what is meant is the Primordial Tradition itself, but the return of the Golden Age now belongs less to the past than to the next cycle of time. Clearly the "occidentation" of the Dunites was bereft of traditional understanding.

Regardless, the phenomenon of the Dunites recalls that other expression of apocalyptic California, *Dune* by Frank

---

[155] Beorse, op. cit., page 37.
[156] On this derivation and the importance of Lemuria in the modern understanding of Mount Shasta, see *The Red and the White*, page 45, and *Guardians of the Heart*, page 52.

Herbert. I have explored the inspirations for Herbert's novel in *Mysteries of Dune*, as well as its specific relationship to San Francisco, a place named for the mission dedicated to Saint Francis himself. According to the doctrines of Islamic esoterism, the "region of the dunes" (*al-Kathīb*) is a realm of Divine disclosure belonging to the posthumous states;[157] in other words, it properly belongs to the "lands of the dead." In the San Francisco Bay Area there are other missions, and other paths of the dead,[158] yet hopes for a final reversal haunt both the example of the Dunites and the imaginary world of *Dune*. The latter, however, is centered upon an intervention of a transcendent principle in the form of its hero, who is explicitly identified as al-Mahdi.[159]

California is known as the Golden State due to a darker side of its history; yet every symbol has both a luminous as well as a tenebrous aspect. Long before the darkness of the Gold Rush, California was illuminated by the symbolism of the Golden Age; Garci Rodríguez de Montalvo's described the island as "very close to the site of the Terrestrial Paradise." Going to California has ever since constituted a sort of pilgrimage, whether for gold or for Disneyland, but every

---

[157] See Corbin 1977, page 150.

[158] It may be offered that the greatest researcher of ancient science in the Bay Area was attached to Mission San Jose in Fremont, although her religious superiors were not supportive of her work (see "Some Remarks on the 'Mystery Walls,'" op. cit.).

[159] Certain particulars of Herbert's original novel might further be compared with the themes in this study, in particular the relationship of the hero Paul Atreides with the Bene Gesserit. Herbert modelled this Sisterhood loosely upon another Catholic order, the Jesuits, and though the number 9 is not emphasized, there is no question that inasmuch as Paul the son of Leto recalls an Apollonian function, the Bene Gesserit suggest the Muses; perhaps even more so, the Bene Gesserit "witches" recall the Nine Witches of Caer Lloyw who first train and then oppose the hero.

pilgrimage is really a path to sainthood or it is folly; the Golden State must really be the primordial state, or it is made of fool's gold. At present, people know more about Disney princesses than the power of the Nine Sisters. "California Dreamin'" has taken the place of prayer for many, while the rise of megachurch Christianity has eclipsed more traditional forms.[160]

Even if the historic catastrophe that befell Native civilization was not the apocalypse, it was obvious to Native and Franciscan alike that the ending of the world was near. Islam as the final revelation insists on the participation of Jesus at the End of Time with symbolism that is solar. Leaving aside exoteric differences, it should be admitted that this Islamic formulation is essentially identical to the solar Christ venerated in the California missions. From this point of view, and to look at the admittedly dim "bright side," the padres did indeed serve as "gatekeepers of the impending apocalypse" for California, for just as the Caliph of God prepares the faithful for the return of Jesus, the "land of the Caliph" was in some measure prepared by the Franciscans for that return.

Along the western edge of the world, the California missions still stand like ghosts from another time, pointing to a time that according to the "Prophecy of the Popes" is now within sight. Despite the apparent absence of "gatekeepers" at the missions or upon Morro Rock - or perhaps because of this state of affairs – California is finally ready for the arrival of a western sunrise.

---

[160] Among other things, evangelical Christianity advocates support for the state of Israel; this countertraditional position at once parodies the companionship of Moses and Jesus at the Transfiguration and rejects the rapprochement of traditional Christianity and Islam that is the special concern of the Custodians of the Holy Land.

www.ingramcontent.com/pod-product-compliance
Lightning Source LLC
Chambersburg PA
CBHW041649170426
43195CB00043B/2975